INSTANT LESSONS

FOR SUPPLY TEACHERS

Candy Adler

5-7

YEARS

A & C Black • London

Dedicated to my Mum who would have been so proud!

I would like to personally thank the following people for their contributions to this book in one way or another:
My son, Lee; My lovely Dad, Arnie, and Gill; Pat Woodcock-Howes; Sharon Laming – la mia amica bella; the very talented Katie Collins; Deputy Head and teacher extraordinaire, Koula Christofides-Quinn; Alan Cocker and all the staff and children at Cranborne Primary School, Potters Bar, Herts; Laura Schofield at Capita Education Resourcing (Luton branch); Dawn King; Lindsey White; Michelle Collins; Sylvia Borrows, Ann Limbrick; Bob, Mandy and Alan at the Cock o' the North, Bell Bar, Herts for all the cappuccini, backchat, laughter, encouragement and allowing me to spread my work all over the tables; everyone else who has helped me along the way.

Published 2009 by A & C Black Publishers Limited
36 Soho Square, London W1D 3QY
www.acblack.com

ISBN 978-1-4081-1157-4

Copyright text: © Candy Adler 2009
Copyright illustrations: © Catherine Ward 2009
Copyright cover illustration: © KJA Artists 2009
Editor: Margot O'Keeffe
Designed by: Blade Communications
CD-ROM designed and developed by Cambridge Digital (www.cambridgedigital.com); produced by Will Burrows

A CIP catalogue record for this book is available from the British Library.

The author and publishers gratefully acknowledge permission to reproduce the following copyright material:

Shutterstock for:
Wrap It Up! Wedding (389465) Jennifer Lynn Arnold; Football (1632140) John Rawsterne; Christmas (2174057) Linda Webb; Any celebratory occasion (14476132) M Jackson; New Baby Girl (18040090) Erica Truex

What Fruit or Vegetable Am I? Aubergine (11167312) Valentyn Volkov; Kiwi (25620499) Marylooo; Bean 2 (20268850) Cameramannz ; Melon (10838074) Elena Schweitzer; Raspberry (8482240) Valentyn Volkov; Pepper (24801460) Yellowj; Courgette (9132289) Elena Schweitzer; Leek (24529945) Zaneta Baranowska

Where in the World? Duram wheat (6113206) Tyler Olson; Sugar beet (2120586) Marek Pawluczuk; Sugar cane (1594576) IRP; Pasta (22101292) Iwona Grodzka;

Jar of sweets (1316871) Christophe Testi; Marmalade (11801596) Elzbieta Sekowska; Bun with heart (23684701) stocknadia; Biscuits (19653091) Monkey Business Images; Chocolate (14124292) Cre8tive Images; Tin of pineapple (8881558) mironenkomihail; Bread (24925660) Pixelbliss; Corn (4937347) Andriy Doriy; Easter egg (20706610) Charlene Bayerle

Can You Recycle? Drinking (452412) Ragne Kabanova; Box (2802064) prism68; Bank (17567743) ZQFotography; Compacted cans (1075159) Michael Plotczyk; Factory (10685911) Photoroller; Recycled can (16258279) Tania Zbrodko

The Animals Went In Two-By-Two reproduced by permission of A&C Black Publishers. Engineered and arranged by James Bachmann, Vocals Sara Shevlin and Andrew White

Every effort has been made to trace copyright holders and to obtain their permission for use of copyright material. The author and publishers would be pleased to rectify any error or omission in future editions.

Printed and bound in Great Britain by Caligraving Ltd, Thetford, Norfolk

A & C Black uses paper produced with elemental chlorine-free pulp, harvested from managed sustainable forests.

Contents

Instant Lessons for Supply Teachers

The job of the supply teacher is one of the most challenging in education. Supply teachers are expected, at short notice, to enter a classroom full of unfamiliar pupils and to deliver inclusive lessons that take account of pupils with differing abilities and that engage them all in worthwhile, curriculum-relevant learning experiences.

The *Instant Lessons for Supply Teachers* series offers a bank of lesson plans and reproducible resources across the curriculum, which can be used at a moment's notice by teachers providing emergency cover. There are three books, one each for 5–7 year olds, 7–9 year olds and 9–11 year olds. Each of these provides 30 lesson plans – 10 Literacy, 10 Mathematics and 10 spread across the other areas of learning (Science, History, Geography, Art, Design, Music, PE and PSHE).

Each book is accompanied by a CD-ROM with all the resources needed – ready-to-print, so there's no need to carry around multiple books and bulky materials. In addition, the CD-ROMs contain PowerPoint versions of all the lesson plans so they can be displayed for whole-class use on an interactive whiteboard.

About the books

Each book contains:
- An introduction explaining how the resources are organised.
- Practical tips and essential information for supply teachers.
- A lesson-plan for each of the 30 lessons. Each of these is presented in a unique and easy-to-use grid format.

The lessons are not numbered as it is not intended that they should be done in a specific order, but rather that they should be dipped into and chosen as appropriate to the needs of the class. It is envisaged that each lesson will take about one hour unless otherwise stated.

- One of the reproducible sheets that accompany the lesson, to give you a glimpse, as you read the lesson plan, of how the resources support the lesson. That sheet as well as all other sheets can be found on the CD-ROM.
- Answers, as appropriate, to lesson-plan activities.

Overview of the CD-ROMs

For each lesson in the book, the CD-ROM contains:
- A PowerPoint presentation of the lesson plan for using on an interactive whiteboard
- The Lesson-Plan Grid
- A list of Success Criteria
- Reproducible and customisable Resource and Activity Sheets
- Where appropriate, colour Resource Sheets for display on an interactive whiteboard
- For some lessons (e.g. Music, PE/Dance), audio files of music
- Some Generic Resources for general use within the Maths section
- The pages of this book as a PDF for viewing and printing out.

For further information, please see page 6 'How to use the CD-ROM'.

Sample lesson-plan grid

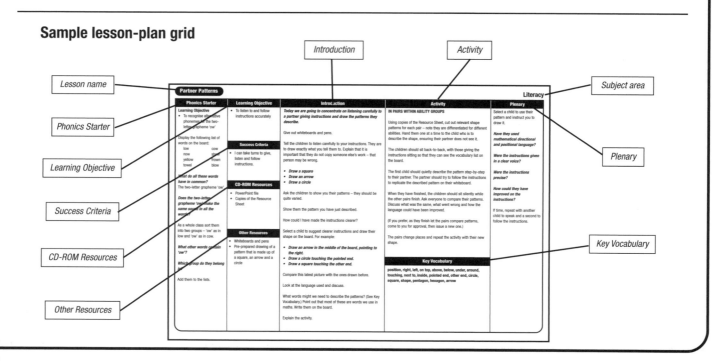

The lesson-plan grids (see facing page)

Each grid provides:

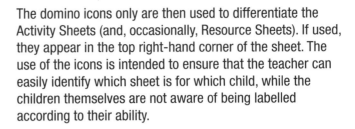

- Learning Objective/s
- Success Criteria
- A list of the CD-ROM Resources required
- A list of Other Resources required
- An Introduction to the lesson, to be used with the whole class
- Description of the group, paired or individual Activity for different levels of ability
- A Key Vocabulary word bank
- Ideas for a Plenary session

In addition:

- All Mathematics lesson-plan grids have a Mental Starter section.
- All Literacy lesson-plan grids in *Instant Lessons for Supply Teachers 5-7 Years* have a Phonics Starter section.

Differentiation

Where relevant, ideas are provided for differentiating the content of the lesson to suit the needs of the different abilities in a class. When differentiation by task is suggested, the notes in the Activity section of the lesson-plan grid are organised under the following headings with accompanying domino icons:

AA
The suggestions here are for children with an above average ability, or at the top end of the book's age range.

MA
The suggestions here are for children of average ability, or in the middle of the book's age range.

LA
The suggestions here are for children of lower ability, or at the lower end of the book's age range.

SEN
Usually the children with Special Education Needs are given the same task as the LA children. However, occasionally added support for these children is necessary.

The domino icons only are then used to differentiate the Activity Sheets (and, occasionally, Resource Sheets). If used, they appear in the top right-hand corner of the sheet. The use of the icons is intended to ensure that the teacher can easily identify which sheet is for which child, while the children themselves are not aware of being labelled according to their ability.

The reproducible sheets

Activity Sheets
Activity Sheets are those sheets on which the children will be inputting information in some form. This may be writing, completing tables or creating designs and artwork. These sheets are differentiated where possible and this is shown using the dominoes icons described above.

Support Activity Sheets
These sheets are for children who need additional support.

Resource Sheets
Resource Sheets are non-consumable sheets. They are not intended for the children to write on. It is recommended that they are displayed on the whiteboard or enlarged copies printed out and displayed somewhere in the classroom. In some cases, these are provided in full colour. Many of the Resource Sheets are gameboards. In some cases, they are also differentiated so that the children play the game most suited to their ability, even though it has the same objective as the other gameboard(s) for other ability groups. Again, these could be enlarged and laminated. In some cases, the rules are on the gameboard itself and, in other cases, the rules are a separate Resource Sheet to be displayed or for the children to keep with them. It is recommended that you explain or read through any game rules with the children; the reading level of the written rules may not be accessible to all children.

Generic Sheets
The CD-ROM contains a collection of Generic Sheets within the Maths section:

- Number lines: 0–100, 0–50 and 0–20
- Playing cards for the numbers 1 to 10
- Playing cards for the numbers 11 to 20
- Playing cards for the numbers 21 to 30
- Multiplication squares
- 100 squares
- Numbers Word Bank

It would be useful to have these laminated so that they can be used many times, rather than printing off several sheets.

Supply Teacher Feedback Form

The Supply Teacher Feedback Form on page 72 (and also on the CD-ROM) provides a helpful template on which to feed back information to the class teacher. A filled-in exemplar is provided on page 73 of this book.

Answers

Answers to activities are provided as appropriate, both at the back of this book (on pages 74–80) and on the CD-ROM along with the other resources for the relevant lesson unit.

The PowerPoint presentations

The PowerPoint presentations offer you an alternative method of delivering the lesson. As you talk the class through the various points, a frame-by-frame version of the lesson, together with any diagrams or sample sheets needed to demonstrate the activity, is displayed.

You can move down the points by clicking on the screen or using the page down key on the keyboard. Note that a small red + sign indicates that there is more text to follow on that slide.

The Success Criteria sheet features towards the end of the presentation – before the Plenary session – so that it can be left on display for the children to refer to as they work.

How to use the CD-ROM

The CD-ROM included with this book contains an easy-to-use interface that allows to you to print out pages from the book, to view them (e.g. on an interactive whiteboard) or to customise the activities to suit the needs of your pupils.

Getting started

Insert the CD-ROM into your CD drive and the disk should autorun and launch the interface in your web browser. If the disk does not autorun, open 'My Computer' and select the CD drive, then open the file 'start.exe'. If you are using a Mac, select the CD drive and open the 'start.app' file.

Please note: due to the differences between Mac and PC fonts, you may experience some unavoidable variations in typography and page layouts.

Navigating through the CD-ROM

The Home Screen provides links to the following areas of the CD-ROM: the End User Licence Agreement, the Supply Teacher Feedback Form, and the main menu or Contents Page.

Four options are available to you from the Contents page:

1. The first option takes you to the Book PDF, where you can choose pages of the book to view and print out, using Adobe Reader (see below).

2. The second option takes you to the Mathematics lessons resources.

3. The third option takes you to the Literacy lessons resources.

4. The fourth option takes you to the Other Subjects lessons resources.

Click on any of options 2–4 to display a list of the 10 lessons in the relevant section. Then click on a lesson title to display all the resources for that lesson.

There is a 'Back' button in the top right of the Contents screen to return to the Home Screen.

If you do not have the Microsoft Office suite (with Word and PowerPoint), you might like to consider using OpenOffice instead. This is a multi-platform and multilingual office suite, and an 'open-source' project. It is compatible with all other major office suites, and the product is free to download, use and distribute (see www.openoffice.org). Other compatible software includes Ability Office and Star Office. Use an Internet search engine to locate current versions of alternative software.

If you do not already have Adobe Reader (for accessing PDF files) it can be downloaded for free from www.adobe.com.

File formats

You will find four different file formats on the CD-ROM:

- PowerPoint files (PPT) enabling the lessons to be presented on an interactive whiteboard;

- MP3 files containing music tracks for Music and PE/Dance lessons*;

- PDF files of all resources enabling them to be viewed, displayed on an interactive whiteboard or visualiser, and printed;

- WORD files of many of the resources, enabling you to edit and customise the resource – and to print it out, or copy and paste it into your existing planning using Microsoft Word.

*NB: This CD-ROM cannot be used in a CD player. The audio tracks on the CD-ROM are provided in mp3 format. These can be copied from CD or computer onto a media player such as an mp3 player, or copied to a new CD to use in a CD player for personal or educational use. No rights of distribution are granted or implied by this.

Technical support

If you have any question regarding the *Instant Lessons for Supply Teachers* software, please email us at the address below. We will get back to you as quickly as possible.

educationalsales@acblack.com

Example Lesson Resources: Shape Spotting

The following is an example of a lesson with some of the resources provided.

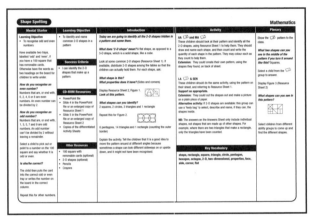

Lesson Plan Grid

Success Criteria Sheet

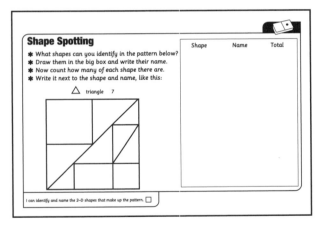

Activity Sheet

Resource Sheet

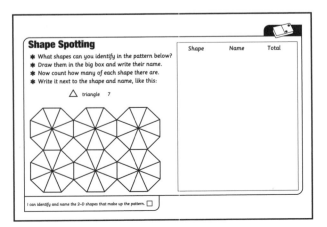

Activity Sheet

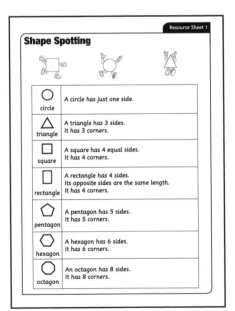

Getting Started

Types of supply-teaching work

There are generally three different types of supply-teaching work available:

- Day-to-day work involves covering sickness, training courses, conferences and so on. In the case of sickness, this type of work usually involves last-minute, early-morning calls. Cover for conferences and training courses is most often pre-booked.

- Longer-term work may involve any cover from a week to a half term (6-8 weeks).

- Fixed contract may involve cover for between a half term to an academic year – to cover long-term sickness, maternity leave and so on.

Ways of getting supply work

Local Education Authority (LEA)

To obtain supply teaching work through your Local Education Authority, you must register with them. The procedure will differ from LEA to LEA. If your work comes via an LEA, you should be paid to scale and have pension options through your relevant county. Payment is usually made through their own payroll. Rules of employment vary between LEAs, so check with whichever covers the areas in which you wish to work for their individual conditions and rules.

Agencies

Before registering with an agency, it is valuable to seek recommendations. Talking to other supply teachers is a good place to start. Additionally, schools often have a favourite agency to which they are loyal, so if you wish to work in particular schools, try to find out which agencies they use. You might wish to register with several in order to get sufficient work. However, be aware that agencies set their own rates of pay and this is usually less than LEAs.

Directly through schools

You can only be employed by a school if you already have an LEA payroll number which requires registration with the LEA.

In all cases, you will need to have a Criminal Records Bureau (CRB) Disclosure form. The LEA, agency or school should be able to advise you on obtaining and completing the form.

Preparation

What do I take to school with me?

- ✔ This book and the accompanying CD-ROM
- ✔ A project file containing hard copies from the CD-ROM of relevant lesson plans, Resource Sheets and Activity Sheets
- ✔ Your CRB form, a photo ID card if you have one and your GTC registration card
- ✔ Bottled water (This is sometimes charged for, as are hot drinks. You should offer to pay for any refreshments you have.)
- ✔ Lunch (although it is often possible to order and purchase a lunch if you do it by break time)
- ✔ A story or poetry book (as a filler or for the end of the day)
- ✔ Coloured pens (check the school's policy on marking the register and children's work)
- ✔ Sticky tack (for the Success Criteria and other display material)
- ✔ Counters and dice for the games
- ✔ Trainers to change into if you have to take a PE lesson
- ✔ A small book to keep details of lesson times, names of the Headteacher and other staff and any other relevant notes for future visits
- ✔ Stickers as a reward for good work or behaviour
- ✔ Timesheet – without it you won't get paid!

When should I arrive?

If you say you are available for work, you should be up and ready to go. Schools really appreciate your arriving early, so estimate how long it will take you to get there and be sure to plan your route. Being prepared before the children arrive is paramount to a successful first impression. Ideally you should aim to arrive at least 30 minutes before the start of school.

What should I wear?

Dress professionally, but comfortably. There is an unwritten dress code, which means that jeans and track suits are not acceptable, unless, of course, you are given prior permission to wear these for PE. Wear footwear that you can take PE in or take trainers with you to change into. If you are female, avoid low necklines and short skirts.

What do I do when I get there?

Not all of the following issues need to be addressed as soon as you arrive. However, if you are able to get there early enough to do so, it will make life a lot easier!

- You will have to sign the visitor's book and offer your CRB and identification.
- You may or may not be shown the staff room and the toilets – if not, ask.
- Check whether there is an interactive whiteboard (IWB) in your classroom. If yes, check that it is connected to a laptop or computer and that it is working. If not, you will need hard copies of everything you need for your lessons.
- Find the timetable. Often there is a copy on the wall for the children. This will tell you what the routines are and what time things like assembly are. You should assume you are to attend.
- Fire drill instructions are usually displayed. Make sure you know where the meeting point is.

If you are not told, ask:

- whether you are on break duty – if the class teacher for whom you are covering is on duty, you will probably be expected to do their duty (a list is usually on a board in the staffroom);
- if you stay in the classroom during wet play or will be relieved;
- whether any planning has been left for you (if it has, read it through so that if there are any problems, you have time to query it and/or use the photocopier);
- whether there are any children of whom you need to be especially aware (e.g. those with SENs or behaviour problems);
- what the school behaviour policy is so that you know how to react to bad behaviour;
- whether there is a bell to indicate the end of morning sessions;
- whether or not you collect the class in the morning/breaks and so on, and if so, from where;
- whether or not you lead children out at the end of the day or wait for parents to collect them.

Many classrooms have a Teaching Assistant (TA) assigned to them for at least part of the day. They are a valuable resource, so use them! Not only will they support your teaching, but they are also a treasure trove of information with regard to the individual children, ability groups, the class, school routines and rules, and, very importantly, where the resources are kept. (Be aware: headteachers often ask teaching assistants for feedback about you!)

What will the school expect of me?

Schools expect a supply teacher who will provide professional teaching cover with the minimum disruption to the class and school routine. If work has been left by the class teacher, then it must be taught. However, there may be occasions where you are unable to do so due to lack of resources required or understanding of the planning. In these incidences, use your own lesson plans, but ensure you note your reasons for doing so and what you taught instead on your feedback form.

In addition to effective teaching, schools will also expect you to:

- be prepared and adaptable – things change rapidly in a school day;
- have good control of the class;
- mark all work taught (see 'Marking', page 11);
- leave feedback for the class teacher (see Feedback Form, page 72);
- leave the classroom tidy, shut all windows and turn off lights, computers and the IWB projector;
- report to the office to have your timesheet signed, and sign out.

Behaviour management

Behaviour management is one of the biggest issues in primary classrooms today. You probably have your own strategies that are tried and tested, and that you use on a day-to-day basis. However, we all have different natures and teaching styles, and every catchment area is slightly different, as is every class temperament. What works with some classes or teachers won't necessarily work with others. You need to be adaptable and try different tactics until you find what works for both you and the individual class. The most important thing to remember, however frustrated or exasperated you may feel, is not to lose your temper or shout. Not only will this not result in effective class control, it is likely to exacerbate the situation, causing more problems.

If you don't enjoy teaching in a school because of continued bad behaviour, you don't need to go back. However, you should see any day through to the end. If it is really bad, then there is nothing wrong with asking for help. Other members of staff will usually be willing to offer advice, recognising that it is more difficult to control the behaviour of children you don't know.

First impressions

Children don't like changes to their routines. They need to feel safe and relaxed to be ready to learn. Show that you are in control but approachable. Preparation is the key. Have some early morning work on the board for when they enter the classroom, to keep them occupied while you are dealing with the inevitable queries and issues that arise first thing. Write the date, 'Good morning' and 'My name is …'. Beneath this write the task; for example, 'How many small words can you make out of this word: impossible?' Other tasks might be practising spellings/ tables or writing as many number sentences as possible for a chosen number (choose according to ability).

Establishing your expectations from the outset

- Smile but be authoritative when you speak.
- Select sensible children to help you with any important morning jobs, such as taking the register to the office.
- Appoint a helper of the day.
- Lay down your main class rules as soon as possible and give the children a clear idea of your expectations for the day.
- Request silence for the register, and ask the children to respond to their name by answering and giving a little wave so that you can put a face to the name.

Making it personal

The sooner you know the children's names, the better. This puts them at ease and helps with class control. Try giving each child a sticky label with their name on it to wear. Your teaching assistant may be able to find the sticky labels and do this for you. Or you can carry some in your supply kit, just in case. Alternatively, you could give the children an A4 sheet of paper to fold horizontally and write their first names in large, clear letters so that you can see it from the front of the class.

Putting them at their ease

We all like to know what we are likely to be doing for the day, so tell the children what you have planned. Try to praise them often as possible. Comment on how patiently children are sitting or waiting to speak and acknowledge the efforts some children make in trying to answer a question even if the answer is wrong. Good behaviour that is being noticed and rewarded can be contagious!

Remember to give the children 'settling in' time. Many of them will try to test you. Equally, many children will be very wary of you; after all, you are an 'unknown quantity'.

Children with special needs

Special needs may range from ADHD to dyslexia, dyspraxia, autism and learning difficulties. The

Headteacher or other staff will usually make a point of providing you with information on such children. These children will need activities that are related to what the other children in the class are doing but at their ability level so they can achieve success like everyone else. If their needs are very different, there is usually a Learning Support Assistant (LSA) to support them. They can be a great help in adapting your suggested activities. By all means give special needs children jobs to boost their self-esteem, but sometimes it is just giving them the correct level of work that can produce the best behaviour, especially if it is really interesting to them.

Sanctions

Be aware of the school's behaviour and sanctions policy. Don't make threats you can't carry out or the children will not take the threat seriously next time. Make sure that the children know your expectations regarding behaviour and aim to keep them high but in a positive way.

Stop, look and listen

Children like to chat when they are supposed to be working and the noise level in a classroom needs to remain at a workable level. If a teacher becomes louder to make her/himself heard, the children tend to get louder still. Shouting (unless you have a reason to be very angry) is never successful.

Some useful strategies are:
- Say quietly 'If you can hear me, put your hand on your head'. It is surprising how quickly the class catches on!
- Try touching your head, then shoulders and so on. Children are quick to copy you, thereby helping you to gain whole-class attention in a short time.
- Use an instrument, such as a shaker, tambourine or little drum, to catch the class' attention.
- Try using signs: for example, an ear for 'listen', a red traffic light for 'stop talking', dimming or turning the lights on or off to get children's attention.
- Standing with arms folded, exaggeratedly looking at the clock or watch, until silence prevails can take quite a while, but it does work.
- Use a timer, counting up. Explain, 'If you waste my time, I'll waste yours. This is coming out of your break/lunchtime.' It is amazing how quickly it works. Always give them a chance to earn the time back!

Explain activities and keep children on task

It is important to position yourself in the classroom so that all the children can see you (and you them). When explaining a task, ask several children to repeat it. Be aware that some children with special educational needs might need instructions simplified and given one at a time. They may not be able to remember a list.

Set a time limit in which to complete work. Again, the timer could be used for this. If you are not working with a particular group, circulate around the classroom, commenting on good work or application, and helping where needed. If children have their hands up for help and you are already helping someone, tell them to ask their study partner/work buddy/person sitting next to them for help, and that you will be over shortly.

Serious incidents

Any serious incidents should be reported to the Headteacher or Deputy Head, whether they be behavioural or something a child has disclosed to you in confidence. In the case of the latter, do not encourage the child by asking questions and do not, under any circumstances, show a reaction or promise not to tell anyone else.

Do not restrain fighting children. Try blowing a whistle to shock them to attention, and send another child for help, according to the school policy, in order to protect yourself from allegations and from injuries. In the case of a child who is behaving in a way that might endanger any of the children, act in accordance with the school policy. In the absence of that, usher the rest of the class out to the nearest classroom. Under no circumstances should you make any bodily contact with a child when reprimanding them. This could be interpreted as assault, even if you have only touched their arm.

Safety issues

In order to keep the children and yourself safe while working in a school, remember:

- to be familiar with and follow the school guidelines if there is a fire;

- to follow safety guidelines during P.E. lessons – for example, children should:

    – remove all jewellery and cover any earrings that cannot be removed;

    – wear shoes when walking to and from the hall;

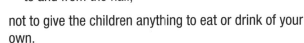

- not to give the children anything to eat or drink of your own.

Assessment

A supply teacher undertaking long-term cover is likely to have been given the class teacher's planning to follow and will be expected to carry out more detailed assessments. The lessons in this book are intended for use when doing varied daily supply teaching, so the only assessment will be during the lesson with questioning and marking the work. Assessment for learning, or formative assessment, is diagnostic, usually oral, through asking questions and discussion. It is already present in the lesson plans in this book in the form of key questions within the Introduction and Plenary sessions. As you circulate, ask children specific questions about their work, for example: How did you know that? How did you get that answer? How did you work that out? What strategy did you use? Why do you think that is? What do you think you need to do next?

Don't forget to praise and give constructive feedback to move the children forward in order that they make progress.

Assessment of learning, or summative assessment, will be carried out primarily through marking. The 'I can...' success-criteria statements at the bottom of most Activity Sheets are intended for children to complete themselves to support self-assessment.

Marking

All work must be marked – it is part of your job and is usually incorporated into the contract you signed. Marking must be finished before you leave the class.

All schools have a marking policy, often displayed on the wall for the children. A glance through the books will tell you how the teacher marks and in what colour. Only mark to the learning objective set. If it is to write rhyming couplets and the couplets don't rhyme, then the learning objective has clearly not been achieved. You may wish to correct a few of the most commonly misspelled words. Maths and literacy should include a comment to help the children improve. For example, if, when marking co-ordinates, the child has omitted brackets, you could write: 'Good work, X, but remember to place brackets round each set of co-ordinates.'

What do I do at the end of the day?

✔ Leave time at the end of the day so that the children can clear up.

✔ Ask the children whether they stack the chairs, put them up on the tables or leave them.

✔ Complete any marking.

✔ Fill in the Feedback Form (see page 72)

✔ Check that the computers and projector are turned off, close the windows and turn out the lights.

✔ Get your timesheet signed, sign out and, if appropriate, give some verbal feedback to the Headteacher or secretary.

Simply Sorting

Mental Starter	Learning Objective	Introduction	Activity	Plenary

Learning Objectives

- To count on and back in twos
- To recognise odd and even numbers

Ask the children to count on in twos from 0 to 50 and back.

Are these numbers odd or even?

What tells us if a number is an even number?
Numbers that are, or end with, 0, 2, 4, 6 or 8 are even numbers. An even number can be divided by 2.

What tells us if a number is an odd number?
Numbers that are, or end with, 1, 3, 5, 7 and 9 are odd numbers. An odd number can't be divided by 2 without leaving a remainder.

Learning Objective

- To sort objects to one or two criteria

Success Criteria

- I can sort objects into two boxes in a sorting diagram.

CD-ROM Resources

- PowerPoint file
- Copies of the differentiated Activity Sheets
- Answers Sheets

Other Resources

- Scissors
- Glue
- Sticky tack
- Compare Bears (or multi-link cubes)

Introduction

Today we are going to sort objects first by one criterion (rule) and then two criteria.

Place two large hoops on the floor, one labelled 'blue' and the other 'not blue'. Select 12 children to choose a 'Compare Bear' or multi-link cube of different colours and stand outside the hoops.

How can we sort the bears?

Ask the children to place their bears/cubes in the correct hoop.

What can you say about the first hoop? They are all blue.

What can you say about the second hoop? They are any colour except blue.

Repeat this using 'red' and 'not red'.

Now we are going to use a sorting diagram to sort objects.

wearing a sweatshirt	not wearing a sweatshirt

Select a few children who fit one of the criteria and ask them to write their names in the correct boxes.

How can we use this diagram to sort objects using two criteria?

Add another set of boxes and another criterion.

	wearing a sweatshirt	not wearing a sweatshirt
wearing trousers		
not wearing trousers		

Who is wearing both a sweatshirt and trousers?
Who is not wearing a sweatshirt but is wearing trousers?

Repeat for all combinations and fill in some names of children.

Repeat this using criteria: numbers less than 10 and odd numbers, using 1 – 16 inclusive.

Explain the activity.

Activity

AA
These children should use the two criteria to sort the numbers and then copy them into the correct box. They should then repeat this using words. (Remind them that the vowels are a, e, i, o, u.)

MA
These children should also use two criteria to sort numbers and then copy them into the correct box. In this case the numbers are all less than 100. Remind the children how to decide if a number is even or odd. They should repeat the activity using the names of parts of the body.

LA & SEN
You might wish to enlarge the Activity Sheet to A3 for these children to make cutting out easier for them. They should cut out the pictures of different objects relating to transport and sport and paste them into the correct boxes. **Support as appropriate.**

Key Vocabulary

count on, count back, odd, even, numbers, units, sort, diagram, select, label, multiples, less than

Plenary

Explain to the children that they are going to sort numbers into a sorting diagram.

Work through task on the board as a whole class.

Is the number even?

Is the number less than 50?

Which section does it belong in?

Where does the number go if it is even and is less than 50?

Ask different children to sort one number each into the sorting diagram until it is complete.

Simply Sorting

Numbers: 78 37 21 6 64 28 50 45 15 42 53 61

Words: glasses arm mouth nose leg chin ankle sock watch ear knee eyebrow elbow

	even numbers	not even numbers
less than 50		
not less than 50		

	parts of the body	not parts of the body
on the face		
not on the face		

I can sort using 2 criteria (rules). ☐

Take Two and Total

Mental Starter	Learning Objective	Introduction	Activity	Plenary
Learning Objective • To recall pairs with a total of 10/20. Write 10 on the board. ***What pairs of numbers can you think of that, when added together, make 10?*** Write them on the board as a spider diagram. Repeat this for 20. ***What strategies did you use?*** Discuss the children's strategies.	**Learning Objective** • To recall pairs of numbers that total 20 (number bonds) **Success Criteria** • I can add pairs of numbers that add up to 20. **CD-ROM Resources** • PowerPoint file • Copies of Generic Sheets 2–4 (Number Cards) **Other Resources** • Whiteboards and pens • Multi-link cubes or similar for LA and SEN	***Today we are going to play a pairs card game where all the cards must add up to 20.*** ***How can we work out the pairs of numbers that make 20, using the knowledge we have of pairs of numbers that make 10?*** Discuss place value. ***Using the units that we already have, what ways can we change these numbers to make 20?*** By adding 10 to one of the numbers. Model the possibilities of 5 + 5 on the board – 15 + 5 and 5 + 15. ***So, we know that 7 + 3 = 10. How can we use that to make a calculation that totals 20?*** Either 17 + 3 or 7 + 13. ***So, what is the rule for making the pairs of numbers total 20 instead of 10?*** Add 10 to one of the two numbers. ***Does it matter which number we add 10 to?*** ***Can you tell me a pair of numbers with a total of 20?*** Write them on board. ***Using the same strategy, can you tell me some pairs of numbers that total 30?*** ***What about pairs of numbers that total 40?*** Explain the activity.	**IN PAIRS, WITHIN ABILITY GROUPS** • Two players take turns to play. One plays, the other checks. • Each keeps their own score. • They spread the cards upside down on the floor or a table and mix them up. • Player 1 selects two cards, adds and says the answer out loud. Player 2 checks that the answer is correct. • See ability group notes below for how to score. • The winning player has the most points. **AA** This group should use Cards 1–29 (Generic Sheets 2–4). They should play the game, trying to make a total of 30 with their two cards. If the addition is correct, they score 1 point. If it is correct and the total is 30, they score 2 points. **MA** This group should use Cards 1–19 (Generic Sheets 2 and 3). They should play the game, trying to make a total of 20. If their addition is correct, they score 1 point. If the cards add up to 20, they score a bonus point. **LA & SEN** This group should use Cards 1–10 (Generic Sheet 2). They should play the game, trying to make a total of 10. They could play in teams if you wish. If they are correct, they keep the cards. The player/team with the most cards wins. Let them use counting aids to help them. **Support as appropriate.**	Play 'Make 20 Bingo'. The children should draw a 3 x 2 grid on their whiteboards and write random numbers from 1–19 (or 1–9 if preferred) in the squares. Give help where necessary. Call out random numbers from 1–19 (or 1–9). If the children have a number that, when added to the number you called out, makes 20, they should cross that number out. If they are all crossed out, they shout 'Made 20!'.

Key Vocabulary

pairs, numbers, add together, total, strategies, number bonds, ten, twenty, thirty

Success Criteria

I can add pairs of numbers that add up to 20.

✔ I can use what I know about pairs of numbers up to 10 to help me.

✔ I can add a 10 to one of the numbers to make 20.

5 + 5 = 10   15 + 5 = 20   5 + 15 = 20

Fairytale Survey

Mental Starter

Learning Objective
- To count on and back in steps of 10

Ask the children to count on and back in tens from 10 – 200.

What changes each time we count on or back?

Write a sequence of numbers on the board with one missing, such as:
47, 57, ___, 77, 87.

Which number is missing?

Repeat with other missing numbers.

Learning Objective

- To answer a question by collecting information and recording it in a block graph

Success Criteria

- I can answer a question by collecting information and recording it in a block graph.

CD-ROM Resources

- PowerPoint file
- An enlarged copy of any one of the differentiated Activity Sheets for display
- Copies of the differentiated Activity Sheets

Other Resources

- Pencils

Introduction

Today we are going to answer the question 'Which fairytale do we prefer?' and record the results on a graph.

How can we answer this question?

By asking each other and collecting information/answers. Explain that this is called a 'survey'.

Write on the board the titles of each fairytale and draw a box at the side of each one.

Explain to the children that they have a choice of six fairytales to choose from. They must decide which story is their favourite. Once they have decided on one, they must stick with it! Point to the list on the board and read through the choices: Cinderella, Little Red Riding Hood, Jack and the Beanstalk, The Three Little Pigs, The Ugly Duckling, Goldilocks and the Three Bears.

Allow them a minute of discussion with the child sitting next to them and then to make their choice.

Which is your favourite fairytale out of this choice of six?

Ask each child to say the name of their favourite. Make a tally mark for each child by each title of their choice.

How many preferred Cinderella?

Count the number of tallies and write the total number beside them.

How can we show this information so that it is easier to answer the question: Which fairytale do we prefer?

On a block graph.

Display the block graph from an Activity Sheet. Tell the children this type of graph is called a block graph.

How do we complete a block graph?

Demonstrate this on the board.

Explain the activity.

Activity

Show the children their sheets. Explain that the block graph had to be on its side on the sheet so there could be enough room for up to 30 children. They will need to turn the sheet round, when they have completed the grid, to answer the questions.

AA 🁣

These children should label the blank block graph with the fairytale titles, and then complete it using the collated information on the board. They should then answer the questions on their Activity Sheet, using the completed graph to find the answers. Finally, they should devise and write a question using the information on the graph.

MA 🁣

These children should complete the block graph using the collated information on the board. They should then answer the questions beneath the graph, using the completed graph to find the answers.

LA 🁣 **& SEN**

These children should complete the block graph using the collated information on the board. They should then answer the questions, using the completed graph to find the answers. **Support as appropriate.**

Key Vocabulary

counting on, counting back, steps, tens, sequence, record, collect information, tick, most, least, total, survey, block graph

Plenary

As a whole class, ask the children to look at their block graphs and answer the following questions.

How can we tell, from our graphs, which fairytale we prefer?

The highest shaded block.

From your graphs, which is the fairytale we prefer?

How can we tell, from our graphs, which fairytale we prefer least?

The lowest shaded block.

From your graphs, which fairytale was liked the least?

Share some of the questions that the 🁣 group made up and ask the other groups to answer them, using their block graphs.

Fairytale Survey

Which fairytale do we prefer?

	30						
	29						
	28						
	27						
	26						
	25						
	24						
	23						
	22						
	21						
	20						
	19						
	18						
	17						
	16						
	15						
	14						
	13						
	12						
	11						
	10						
	9						
	8						
	7						
	6						
	5						
	4						
	3						
	2						
	1						

Cinderella | Little Red Riding Hood | Jack and the Beanstalk | The Three Little Pigs | The Ugly Duckling | Goldilocks and the Three Bears

Which fairytale did we prefer? _____

Which fairytale did we like the least? _____

How many children like The Ugly Duckling best? _____

I can answer a question by collecting information and recording it in a block graph. ☐

Shape Spotting

Mental Starter	Learning Objective	Introduction	Activity	Plenary

Learning Objective
- To recognise odd and even numbers

Learning Objective
- To identify and name common 2-D shapes in a pattern

Success Criteria
- I can identify the 2-D shapes that make up a pattern.

CD-ROM Resources
- PowerPoint file
- Slide 4 in the PowerPoint file or an enlarged copy of Resource Sheet 1
- Slide 5 in the PowerPoint file or an enlarged copy of Resource Sheet 2
- Copies of the differentiated Activity Sheets
- Answers Sheet

Other Resources
- 100 square with removable cards (optional)
- 2-D shapes (optional)
- Pencils
- Crayons

Mental Starter

Have available two trays, labelled 'odd' and 'even', if you have a 100 square that has removable cards.

Otherwise have the words as two headings on the board for children to write under.

How do you recognise an even number?

Numbers that are, or end with, 0, 2, 4, 6 or 8 are even numbers. An even number can be divided by 2.

How do you recognise an odd number?

Numbers that are, or end with, 1, 3, 5, 7 and 9 are odd numbers. An odd number can't be divided by 2 without leaving a remainder.

Select a child to pick out or point to a number on the 100 square and say whether it is odd or even.

Is she/he correct?

The child then puts the card into the correct odd or even tray or writes the number on the board in the correct column.

Repeat this for other numbers.

Introduction

Today we are going to identify all the 2-D shapes hidden in a pattern and name them.

What does '2-D shape' mean? A flat shape, as opposed to a 3-D shape, which is a solid shape, like a cube.

Look at some common 2-D shapes (Resource Sheet 1). If available, distribute 2-D shapes among the tables so that the children can actually hold them. For each shape, ask:

What shape is this?
What properties does it have? (Sides and corners)

Display Resource Sheet 2, Figure 1.
Look at this pattern.

What shapes can you identify?
2 squares, 2 circles, 3 triangles and 2 rectangles (counting the outer border)

Repeat this for Figure 2.

6 pentagons, 14 triangles and 1 rectangle (counting the outer border)

Explain the activity. Tell the children that it is a good idea to move the pattern around at different angles because sometimes a shape can look different sideways on or upside down, and it might not have been recognised.

Activity

AA [image] **and MA**

These children should look at their pattern and identify all the 2-D shapes, using Resource Sheet 1 to help them. They should draw and name each shape, and then count and write the quantity of each shape in the pattern. They may colour each as they count to help them.

Extension: They could create their own pattern, using the shapes they found, on back of sheet.

LA [image] **& SEN**

These children should do the same activity, using the pattern on their sheet, and referring to Resource Sheet 1.
Support as appropriate.
Extension: They could cut the shapes out and make a picture on a plain piece of paper.
Alternative activity: If 2-D shapes are available: this group can use a 'feely bag' to select, describe and name, if they can, the shapes inside.

NB: The answers on the Answers Sheet only include individual shapes, not shapes that are made up of other shapes. For example, where there are two triangles that make a rectangle, only the triangles have been counted.

Key Vocabulary

shape, rectangle, square, triangle, circle, pentagon, hexagon, octagon, 2-D, two-dimensional, properties, face, side, corner, flat

Plenary

Show the [image] pattern to the class.

What two shapes can you see in the middle of the pattern if you turn it around like this? Squares.

Select a child from the group to answer.

Display Figure 3 (Resource Sheet 2)

What shapes can you see in this pattern?

Select children from different ability groups to come up and find the different shapes.

Shape Spotting

* What shapes can you identify in the pattern below?
* Draw them in the big box and write their name.
* Now count how many of each shape there are.
* Write it next to the shape and name, like this:

△ triangle 7

Shape	Name	Total

I can identify and name the 2-D shapes that make up the pattern. ☐

Dot-to-Dot Multiples

Mental Starter	Learning Objective	Introduction	Activity	Plenary
Learning Objective • To practise counting on in 2s, 5s and 10s Play Multiples Dance. Everyone faces the whiteboard. To the tune of the Conga, sing the 2 times table (up to 10 x 2). Show the children how to step forward with the right foot on 'One lot of 2 is 2,' then with the left foot to repeat the line. Then sing 'da da da da da da da' while leaning forward and raising and lowering each shoulder in turn, then 'da da da da da da' repeating the action while leaning back. Move on to the next line and repeat. Repeat this for the 5 and 10 times tables.	• To practise counting on in multiples of 2, 5 and 10 **Success Criteria** • I can practise counting on in multiples of 2, 5 and 10. **CD-ROM Resources** • PowerPoint file • Slides 4 and 5 in the PowerPoint file or an enlarged copy of Generic Sheet 7 (Large 100 Square) • Copies of the differentiated Activity Sheets • Copies of Generic Sheets 6 and 7 (100 Squares) **Other Resources** • Pencils	*Today we are going to count on in multiples of 2, 5 and 10, and then use the multiples to complete a dot-to-dot picture.* *What is the pattern when we count in 2s?* Elicit that they are even numbers. Display the 100 square. Show the pattern – odd, even, odd, even. Discuss that even numbers end in 0, 2, 4, 6 and 8. *What comes next after 2 if we are counting on in 2s?* Ask the class to count on in 2s, from 0 to 20 several times, pointing on the 100 square as they count. *What comes next after 5 if we are counting on in 5s? Can anyone see a pattern?* The first digit (tens column) increases (goes up) by 1 every other time. The units digits alternate between 5 and 0. *Can you show me on the 100 square?* Count on in 5s from 0–50 several times. Repeat the process for multiples of 10. *What comes next after 10 if we are counting on in 10s? Can you show me on the 100 square?* Count on in 10s from 0–200 several times. *Can anyone see a pattern?* The first digit (tens column) increases (goes up) by 1. Continue looking for a pattern. (The numbers always end in 0 and are always even.) *How can being able to count on in 2s help us to count on in 4s?* By doubling the 2s. *Can you show me on the 100 square?* Explain the activity.	All the children should complete their dot-to-dot pictures by counting in multiples of the table they are practising, then joining the dots. Point out to them that they are reciting their tables, not just joining the dots. **AA** 🖅 These children's pictures are for counting on in 5s (5–110) and 4s (4–130). **Extension:** They could design their own dot-to-dot for counting in 3s on the back of the sheet. **MA** 🖅 These children are counting on in 5s (5–120) and 10s (10–260). **Extension:** They could try the dot-to-dot for 4s. **LA** 🖅 These children are counting on in 2s (2–20) and 10s (10–240). **Extension:** They could try the dot-to-dots for 5s. **Support as appropriate.** **SEN** 🖅 These children are counting on in 1s (to 10) and 2s (to 20). **Extension:** They could try the dot-to-dot for 10s. **LSA support**	*What is the next even number after 18?* *What is the multiple of 5 before 45?* *What three numbers come next? 25, 30, 35, …* *What is the multiple of 10 before 30? 80? …?* *What three numbers come next? 12, 16, 20, …* Ask the children to count on in multiples of 2s up to the 10th multiple. Repeat for 5s, 10s and 4s.

Key Vocabulary

count on, multiples, lots of, ten, five, 100 square, pattern, digit, increase, goes up, tens, units, column, alternate, every other, even, odd, double

Dot-to-Dot Multiples

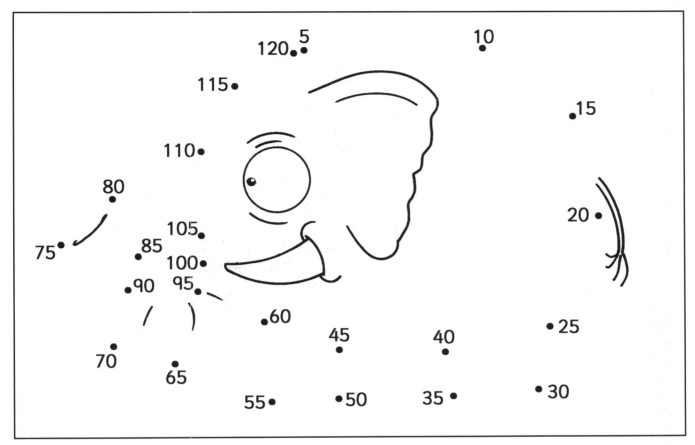

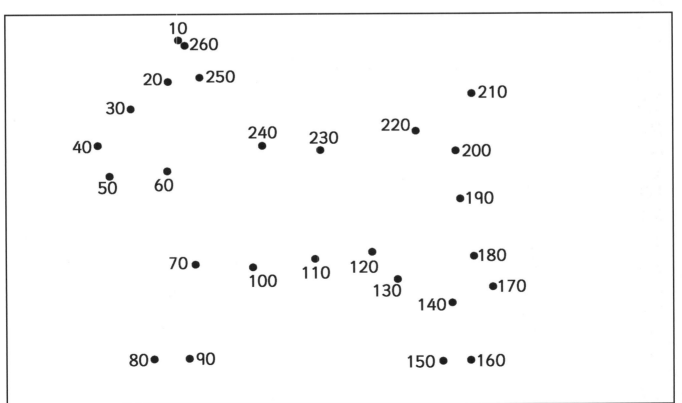

I can count on in 5s and 10s. ☐

Train Doubles

Mental Starter	Learning Objective	Introduction	Activity	Plenary

Learning Objective
- To order the numbers 0–20 on a number line

Draw a number line (without any numbers) on the board. Write in the zero above the first point in the line.

What number should we write on the next point of the line? 1

Select different children to answer and then, if correct, write it on the number line.

Continue until the number line is completely and correctly labelled.

Learning Objective
- To recall the doubles of numbers to 10

Success Criteria
- I can remember the doubles of numbers to 10.

CD-ROM Resources
- PowerPoint file
- Slide 6 in the PowerPoint file or an enlarged copy of Activity Sheet
- Copies of the differentiated Activity Sheets
- Generic Sheets 2 and 3 (Number Cards)

Other Resources
- Crayons

Introduction

Today we are going to play games to help us remember doubles of all numbers up to 20.

What is doubling? 2 lots of (a number).

Tell the children they are going to use their fingers to help them work out the doubles to 10, as we have 10 fingers.

Hold up one finger on each hand and say 'What is double 1?' Model counting the fingers on both hands and say '2. So double 1 is 2.' Ask the children to copy your actions and the words.

Hold up two fingers on each hand and ask 'What is double 2?' 'Double 2 is 4.' Repeat this for 3, 4 and 5.

To reinforce this understanding, ask two children to stand up and ask them each to hold up one finger only. Ask the class to count them with you.

So, double 1 is 2.

Ask those two children to now hold up two fingers each.

What is 2 doubled?

What is 3 doubled?

Repeat this until both children have all their fingers held up.

So, double 10 is 20.

Ensure that the rest of the class is counting and repeating the phrase each time.

Display Slide 6 from the PowerPoint file or an enlarged copy of Activity Sheet.

Explain the activity. Model placing the counter, working out the double and circling the answer.

Activity

The children should play in pairs, within ability groups. MA and LA children should share a gameboard, one using the train at the top, the other the one at the bottom. The AA children will need a gameboard each.
- Shuffle/mix up the number cards.
- Pairs take it in turns to turn over a card.
- They double it and colour in the window of the train containing the correct double of the number turned over.
- Player 2 has their turn.
- If all the cards have been used, shuffle them and use again.
- The winner is the first to have every double circled.

AA
These children should use number cards from 1 to 15.
Extension: Look for a pattern in the doubles in the coloured-in windows. (They are all even numbers.)

MA
These children should use number cards from 1 to 10.

LA
These children should use number cards from 1 to 6.
Support if appropriate.

SEN
These children should carry out the activity using using cards 1 to 12, but using different colours of multi-link cubes or similar. For example, if they pick a card with the number 1 on it, they should take one red cube, then double it by adding another red cube.
With support.

Key Vocabulary

double, doubles, doubled, number line, count on, steps, multiply, odd, even, two lots of, twenty

Plenary

Play 'Doubles Bingo'.

The children should draw a 3 x 2 grid and randomly write six numbers between 2 and 20 in the boxes.

Call out a random number between 1 and 10. Explain that the number being called out must be doubled!

If a child has the doubled number in their grid, they should cross it out.

If a child has crossed out all of their numbers, they should call out 'Doubles!'

Check they are correct, and then continue until several children have finished.

Repeat for doubles up to 40 with the children working in pairs, using their fingers if they need to.

Train Doubles

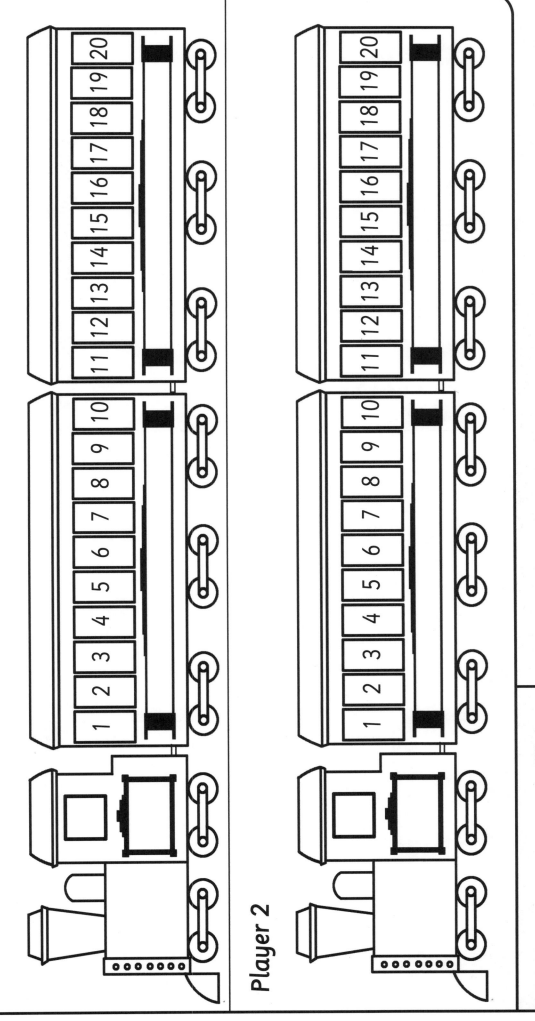

Player 1

Player 2

I can remember all doubles to 20. ☐

Follow My Instructions

Mental Starter

Learning Objective
- To recognise and use whole, half and quarter turns.

Ask the children to stand up and face you.

To check that they know their right hand from their left, ask them to hold up their right hand. Check that all the children are holding up the correct hand. Repeat for their left hand.

Now, issue the following instructions:
- Raise your right hand.
- Shake your left leg.
- Turn a whole turn to your left.
- Turn a half turn to your left.
- Make a quarter turn to your left.

What turn do you need to do to end up facing me again?

Repeat if time, differing the instructions.

Learning Objective

Learning Objective
- To follow and give instructions involving position, direction and movement

Success Criteria
- I can give and follow instructions, using phrases to show position, direction and movement.

CD-ROM Resources
- PowerPoint file
- One copy of Resource Sheet 1 for each group
- Slide 7 in the PowerPoint file or an enlarged copy of Resource Sheet 2
- Copies of the appropriate vocabulary set from Resource Sheet 2

Other Resources
- A large analogue clock to demonstrate
- Squared paper (Extension)

Introduction

Today we are going to give and follow instructions to move an object through a route.

What does route mean? A path taken to get somewhere.

Which way do we turn for clockwise? How do you know? Show the children a quarter turn to the right. Demonstrate on a clock and explain that it is the way a clock turns.

Which way is anti-clockwise? How do you know? Model a quarter turn to the left.

For Year 2:
There is another name for a quarter turn. What is it? A right angle.

Explain that, instead of saying a quarter turn, we will say right angle.

Point out that, to get to the same point, instead of turning three right angles clockwise, we can turn one right angle anti-clockwise.

Draw a simple maze on the board.

Explain to the children that they are going to give instructions to help you work your way through it using the following vocabulary:
Year 1 should use the vocabulary: straight, quarter turns, left and right.

Year 2 should use the vocabulary: straight, right angles, clockwise and anti-clockwise.

Model writing the instructions, numbering each line and beginning on a new line, as you go; for example:
1. Straight;
2. Quarter turn right/right angle turn, clockwise; and so on.

Display Resource Sheet 2 during the activity.

Explain the activity.

Activity

MIXED ABILITY GROUPS
Give each group a copy of the maze (Resource Sheet 1) and the appropriate vocabulary set from Resource Sheet 2.

The children should work as a team. One child should 'walk' their maze, using a Compare Bear, toy car or similar, obeying instructions given by the rest of the group. The 'walker' must only move where directed.

Each instruction given must be agreed on by the rest of the group and must only use the correct mathematical vocabulary.

One of the group should be elected scribe and write down each step of their route, clearly numbered in order, on a separate sheet of paper. They should refer to the relevant word bank (Resource Sheet 2) to help them.

Extension: Using squared paper, groups could draw their own maze and write a set of route instructions.

LA & SEN could have peer support. Adult support where appropriate.

Key Vocabulary

position, direction, route, ¼ turn, quarter turn, ½ turn, half turn, right angle, clockwise, anti-clockwise, instructions, straight line

Year 1 and LA: 'right' and 'left' instead of 'clockwise' and 'anti-clockwise' if they find the concept difficult.

Plenary

Did you manage to get all the way round the maze on your first attempt?

What did you find difficult?

Select one group's instructions and work through them.

Did anyone go wrong at first? Can you show us which way you went?

Follow My Instructions

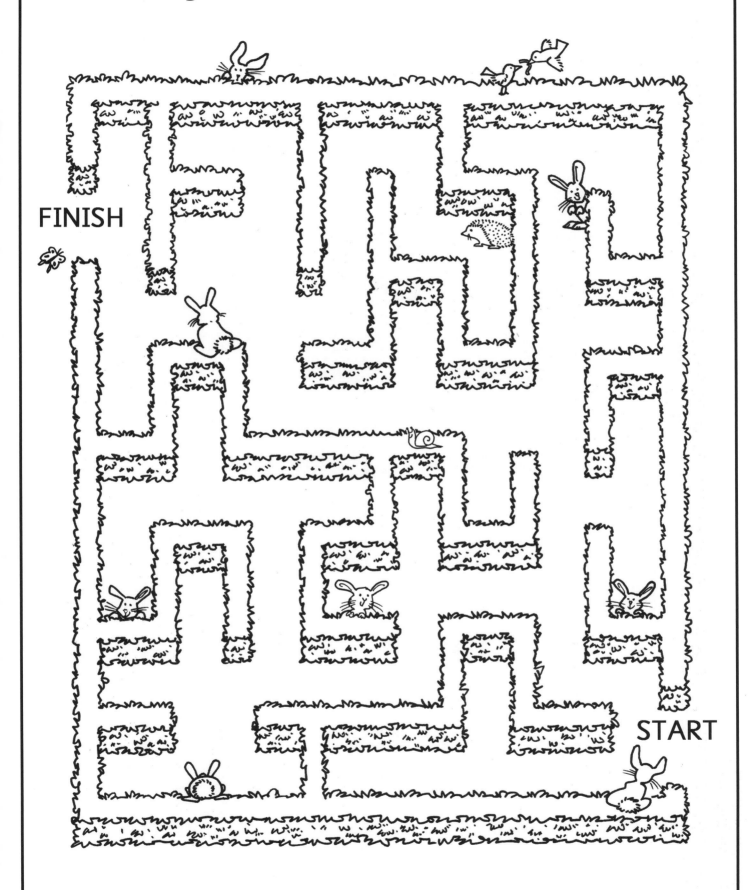

FINISH

START

Toy Shop Game

Mental Starter	Learning Objective	Introduction	Activity	Plenary

Mental Starter

Learning Objective
- To derive and recall subtraction facts for each number to at least 10

Write on the board and say:
5 – 3 = 2

Using five children, model the calculation 5 – 3 = 2. Do this by lining the five children up and removing three of them.

How many are left?

Now change the order to:
3 – 5 = 2

Can we do this? Can we subtract (take away) 5 from 3?

Explain and emphasise that you can change the order of the numbers when adding and get the same answer, but when taking away (subtraction), it doesn't work.

Repeat this for other number sentences, choosing children to demonstrate them, but selecting another child to organise them.

Learning Objective
- To find the difference between two 2-digit numbers in the context of money

Success Criteria
- I can find the difference between two 2-digit amounts of money.

CD-ROM Resources
- PowerPoint file
- Copies of Generic Sheet 1
- Copies of the differentiated Resource Sheets

Other Resources
- Pencils
- Paper or books to write in
- Dice
- Different coloured counters

Introduction

Today we are going to play the 'Toy Shop Game' where you have some money to buy a toy and have to work out how much change you should get.

How can we use a number line to show 5 – 3?

Model this using a number line on the board. Explain that one way to subtract (take away) is to count on from the smaller number to the larger number.

Use other sums subtracting 2-digit numbers from 50p. So if we have 50p and the cost of a toy is 25p, demonstrate how, instead of going one place at a time, we could start on 25p on the number line, jump forward 5 places to 30p, then 10 places to 40p and 10 places to 50p. The number of places we have jumped is 25. So the change we need is 25p.

Tell the children that this is often the way shopkeepers work out the change to give, by counting on from the cost of the item to the money given.

How do we write that as a number sentence?
50p – 25p = 25p

Tell the children that now the amount will increase to £1.

How many pence are there in £1?
How can we show £1 on a number line? (Use a 0–100 number line.)

Ask the children to subtract (take away) 1- and 2-digit numbers from 100.

What is the answer?
How do we write that as a number sentence?

Explain the activity.

Activity

IN PAIRS, IN ABILITY GROUPS
- The players place their counters on START.
- Player 1 throws the dice and moves that many spaces.
- Player 1 then subtracts the amount shown on the square they landed on from the amount of money given, using a number line.
- Player 2 checks that Player 1 is correct. Both write the number sentence down. If correct, Player 1 leaves his or her counter on that square and waits for his or her next turn. If incorrect, Player 1 must go back to START.
- Player 2 has their turn.
- Player 1 throws again, moves on that number of spaces and calculates again.
- The winner is the player who reaches HOME first, or who is nearer to HOME when told to stop playing.

AA

In pairs, these children should use the 0–100 number line (if required) and play the game with £1.00 to buy each item they land on. They should write down £1.00 – cost = ?

MA

In pairs, these children should use the 0–50 number line and play the game with 50p to buy each item they land on. They should write sum 50p – cost = ?

LA & SEN

As a group, led by an adult, these children should play the game using toy money to pay for the toys. Other children should check the amount. (Up to 20p).
Use of 0–20 number line if appropriate.

Key Vocabulary

add, addition, take away, subtraction, pence, p, pounds, £, equals, answer, cost, number sentence, smaller, bigger, difference, pay, change, money, number line, counting back/on

Plenary

Ask the children questions to reinforce and to assess their understanding of subtraction.

I have 50p. How much money would I still have to spend if I lost 10p on the way to the shop?

I have £1. I buy a comic for 70p. How much change will I get back?

Toy Shop Game

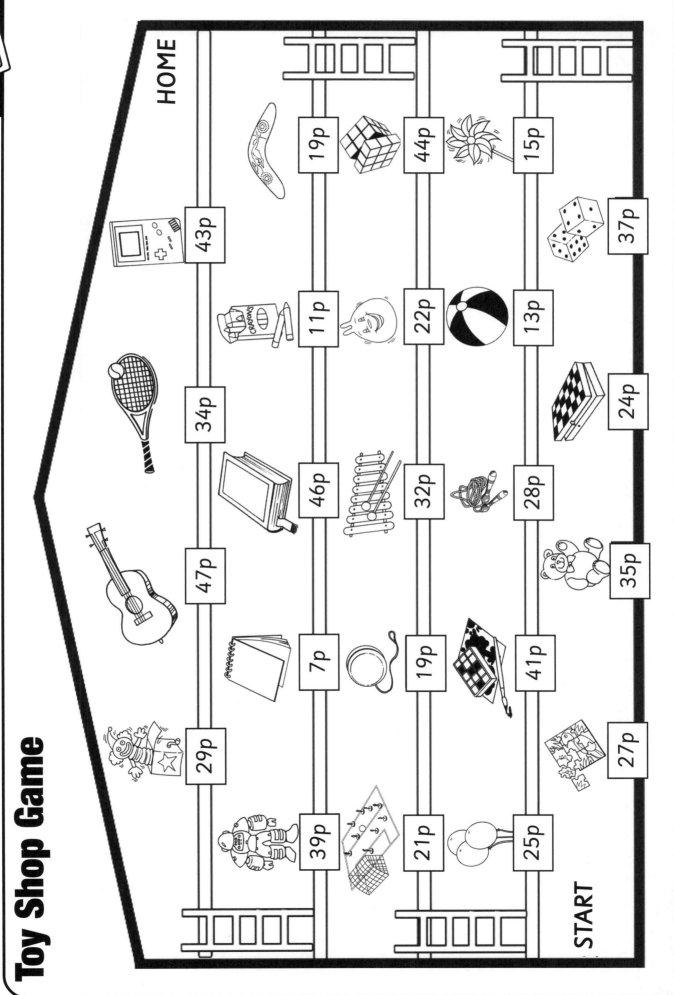

HOME

START

Numbers Mountain Game

28

Mental Starter	Learning Objective	Introduction	Activity	Plenary
Learning Objective • To partition 2- and 3-digit numbers into multiples of 100, 10 and 1 Draw a HTU chart on the board and remind the children what each column represents, giving a concrete example. Using individual whiteboards and pens, the children should draw and label their own HTU columns. Give them a 2-digit number and ask them to partition it on their boards into the columns. On the count of 10 they should all show their answers. Extend this to a 3-digit number. Repeat several times. Now ask the children to make the biggest number they can using 2 digits, then 3 digits.	• To read and write 2-digit and 3-digit numbers in figures and words **Success Criteria** • I can read and write 2-digit and 3-digit numbers in figures and words. **CD-ROM Resources** • PowerPoint file • Copies of the differentiated Resource Sheets • Copies of Generic Sheet 8 (Numbers Word Bank) **Other Resources** • Dice • Different coloured counters • Paper • Pens or pencils • Whiteboards and pens	*Today we are going to play 'Numbers Mountain Game', reading and writing numbers in figures and words.* Explain that numbers greater than nine, but less than 20 have one 10 in them. Write 12 on the board, and then draw a group of 10 and a group of 2. Write some numbers from 0 to 19 in words and figures – the matching ones in different places on the board. *Can you match the numbers in words to figures?* Select different children to do so. *What is a 2-digit number and what are its features?* It always has two digits, such as 50, 34, 97, 52. It contains a multiple of 10 and also a zero or another digit. Write some examples on the board. *What clue do we look for when looking for a number in words that is a multiple of 10?* They end in 'ty'. Show some examples. Write some numbers from 20 to 99 in words and figures – again, the matching ones in different places on the board. *Can you match the numbers in words to figures?* Select different children to do so. Remind the children that, when using hundreds, we don't say 'hundreds' – in the plural. For example, we say 'two hundred', not 'two hundreds'. Explain the activity.	**PAIRS WITHIN ABILITY GROUPS** • Both players place their counters on START at the bottom of the mountain and spiral up towards the top (HOME). • Player 1 throws the dice and moves that many places. If they land on digits, they write these and then the number in words on a piece of paper. If they are words, they write these and then the digits. • Player 2 checks the answer. If it is correct, Player 1 scores 1 point. If incorrect, he or she scores nothing and rewrites correctly beneath the answer. • The winner is the first to reach HOME or the nearest to HOME when asked to stop. • The children should use the Numbers Word Bank to ensure they spell their answers correctly each time. **AA** These children are reading and writing 3-digit numbers. **Extension:** They could make up some questions of their own and challenge a partner to answer them. **MA** These children are reading and writing 2-digit numbers. **Extension:** They could play the 3-digits game (Sheet). **LA & SEN** These children are reading and writing 1- and 2-digit numbers to 20. **Support as appropriate.** **Extension:** They could play the 2-digits game (Sheet) in pairs.	Ask a series of questions using numbers from 0 to 999. Invite children to come up to the board and answer: *What is this number in words?* *What is this number in digits?* Include some 4-digit number questions. *What is 1000 in words?* *How do we say 1054 in words?*

Key Vocabulary

numbers, numerals, figures, digits, ones, units, tens, hundreds, columns, biggest, zero, teens, multiples of ten

Numbers Mountain Game

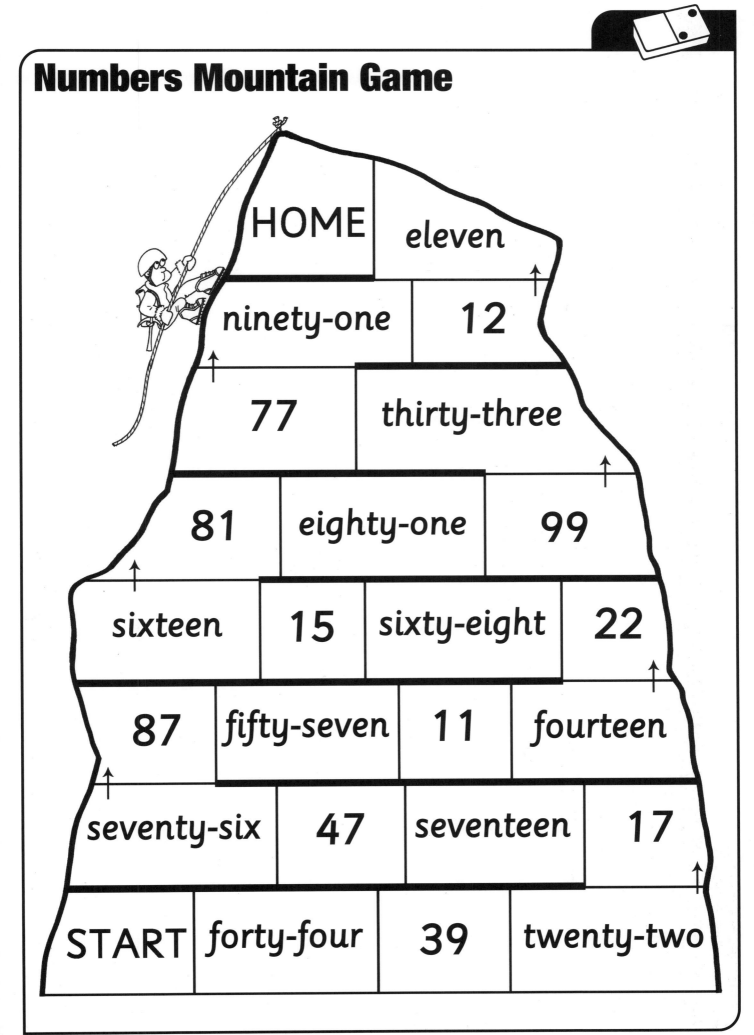

HOME | eleven

ninety-one | 12

77 | thirty-three

81 | eighty-one | 99

sixteen | 15 | sixty-eight | 22

87 | fifty-seven | 11 | fourteen

seventy-six | 47 | seventeen | 17

START | forty-four | 39 | twenty-two

What's the Time? Game

Mental Starter	Learning Objective	Introduction	Activity	Plenary

Learning Objective
- To recognise and use whole, half and quarter turns

Ask the children to stand up and face the whiteboard. Explain that they are going to move clockwise – the way a clock moves. Demonstrate that this is to their right.

Instruct the children to:
- turn a quarter turn
- turn a half turn

What do you need to do to end up facing the front?

Instruct the children to:
- turn a whole turn
- turn a quarter turn
- turn a quarter turn

What do you need to do to end up facing the front?

Repeat this with random turns.

Learning Objective
- To read the time to a quarter of an hour

Success Criteria
- I can read the time to a quarter of an hour.

CD-ROM Resources
- PowerPoint file
- Slides 4, 5, 6 and 8 in the PowerPoint file or a 24-hour analogue clock to demonstrate with
- Copies of the differentiated Resource Sheets
- Copies of the Activity Sheet (Scoring Sheet)

Other Resources
- A large clock
- Small clocks
- Pencils
- Counters
- Dice

Introduction

Today we are going to play 'What's the Time?' – a game where you read the time on a clock.

Show the class a large clock.

What is the long hand called? Hour hand.
What does it show us? Hours.
What is the short hand called? Minute hand.
What does it show us? Minutes.
Which way round do the hands move?
To the right; clockwise, the way the hands move round a clock.

Move the hands on the clock to show some o'clock times.

What is this time? How do you know?
Repeat this several times.

Who can come up and show me 6 o'clock?
Repeat this several times.

What time is it when the minute hand is on the 6? Half past.

Where is the hour hand? It is half way past the hour.

Show how the clock is split in half – past and to – explaining that the hands have travelled half past the hour. Explain that when telling the time, you have to be a detective. The clues are where the minute hand is first, then where the hour hand is.

Move the hands on the clock to show some half past times.

What is the time? How do you know?
Repeat this several times.

Show the quarters of an hour on the clock, explaining a quarter past and a quarter to.

Where is the minute hand for a quarter past?
What do you notice about the hour hand?

Show some quarter past times. Repeat for quarter to, explaining that, as it is not on the 'past' side, it is a quarter to the hour that the hour hand is travelling towards. Give the children some quarter times to identify.

Explain the activity.

IN PAIRS WITHIN ABILITY GROUPS

Rules of the game
- In pairs, the children take it in turns to play *What's The Time?*, using their own copy of the gameboard and a blank scoring board.
- Player 1 throws the dice and moves that number of spaces.
- They then read the time on the clock and write the time in the corresponding space on their blank scoring sheet.
- Player 2 checks the answer. If correct, Player 1 scores one point. If incorrect, they score nothing.
- The winner is the first to reach HOME or until asked to stop.

AA
These children read the time to a quarter of an hour.
Support if appropriate.

MA
These children read the time to a half of an hour.

LA & SEN
These children read the time to the hour.
Support.

NB: On the Activity Sheet, complete the appropriate success criteria for self-assessment before giving the Activity Sheet to the children.

Key Vocabulary

time, clock, minute hand, hour hand, half past, o'clock, quarter to, quarter past, clockwise, half an hour, a quarter of an hour

Plenary

Ask the children random times to show with their arms as the hands.

Show them a range of times on the clock and ask them to say what time it is. Try to target specific children with times at their ability level.

What's the Time? Game

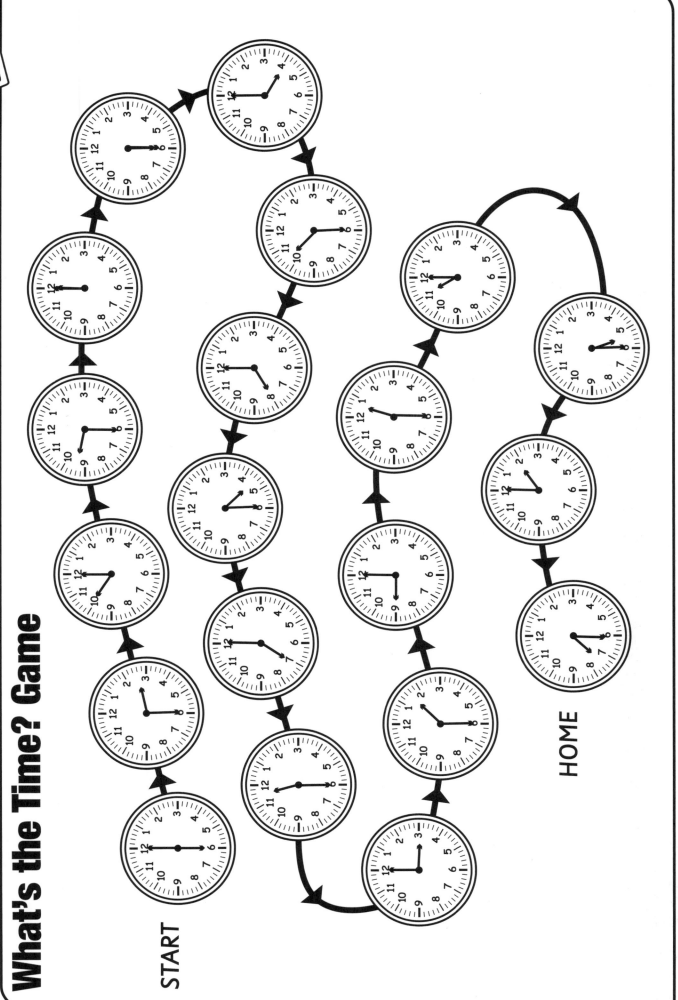

START

HOME

Same Sound Sentences

Phonics Starter	Learning Objective	Introduction	Activity	Plenary
Learning Objective • To learn to spell tricky words Choose some or all of the following tricky words: said, some, come, were, there, when, would, could, should, people, called, their Write the first word on the board and say it aloud. Ask the children to repeat the word. Use the word in a sentence, or ask a volunteer to do so. Ask everyone to repeat the word again and write it in the air, spelling it out as they do so. Finally, ask them to write the word carefully on their whiteboards. Repeat the process with the other words.	**Learning Objective** • To compose and write simple sentences using alliteration **Success Criteria** • I can write same sound sentences. **CD-ROM Resources** • PowerPoint file • Copies of the differentiated Activity Sheets **Other Resources** • Whiteboards and pens • Pencils	*Today we are going to write same sound sentences, using alliteration and action words.* *What is alliteration?* A collection of words that has every word beginning with the same phoneme. Write 'Seven snakes slither.' on the board. *What is an action word?* A doing word (a verb). *Which is the action word in the sentence on the board?* slither *Can you give me some examples of action words?* (dig, jump, jog, sing) Write them on the board underlining the first phoneme. Model some examples; for example, 'Sue sings songs' and 'Dirty dogs dig.' *What sound do these words begin with?* Ask the children to repeat the sounds, s and d, and repeat the sentences. *Can you put the action word 'dig' into another same sound sentence?* Write 'Teddy tickles tummies.' on the board. *What sound do these words begin with?* Ask the children to repeat the sound t and repeat the sentence. Model some longer sentences, emphasising that the sentences must make sense. For example: Carl carelessly crushed cabbage. Sue's sister sneezed suddenly. Dan dutifully dried dirty dishes. Sam started singing sweet songs. *Can you put the action word 'tickles' into a different same sound sentence?* Write some correct suggestions on the board. Explain the activity.	**AA** Independently, these children should make four alliterative sentences using the jumbled up words in the word machine. They should cross out the words in the machine as they use them. Each sentence should contain five words. They should then make up two of their own alliterative sentences using the two words they have not used from the sentence machine. **MA** These children do the same as above, but their sentences only contain four words. They only have one word left over in the machine with which to make up their own same sound sentence. **LA & SEN** Individually or in pairs (whichever is appropriate), but recording independently, these children should make three alliterative sentences using the words in the word machine. Each sentence should contain three words. They should then write one alliterative sentence of their own using the one word not used from the sentence machine. **With support.** **Key Vocabulary** alliteration, sentence, action word, verb, capital letter, full stop, letter, same sound, phoneme, grapheme	Select a child to read their made up sentences. *Which sound was focused on?* Repeat this with as many children as possible (from all ability groups). *Who would like to act out their sentence?*

Same Sound Sentences

✳ Look at the word machine below. There are a lot of words in it.

✳ Make 4 same sound sentences. Use the words in the word machine. Each sentence should contain 4 words.

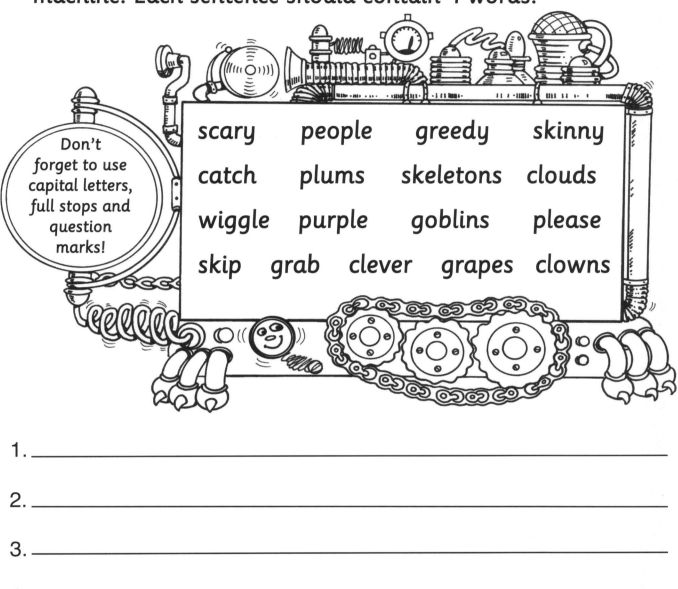

Don't forget to use capital letters, full stops and question marks!

scary	people	greedy	skinny
catch	plums	skeletons	clouds
wiggle	purple	goblins	please
skip	grab	clever	grapes	clowns

1. _____

2. _____

3. _____

4. _____

✳ Which word didn't you use? Use this word to write your own same sound sentence.

_____

I can compose and write same sound sentences. ☐

Word Detective

Phonics Starter	Learning Objective	Introduction	Activity	Plenary

Phonics Starter

Learning Objective
- To practise spelling tricky words

Show the following tricky words:

said, some, come, were, there, when, would, could, should, people, called, their

Display the wordsearch and list of words (Resource Sheet 1).

Who can find one of the tricky words that are in the box?

Select a child to find the word and circle it both in the wordsearch and in the box.

Repeat until completed.

Learning Objective
- To find new and use interesting words and phrases, including story language

Success Criteria
- I can find new and interesting words and phrases.

CD-ROM Resources
- PowerPoint file
- Slide 1 in the PowerPoint file or an enlarged copy of Resource Sheet 1
- Answers Sheet
- Slide 4 in the PowerPoint file or an enlarged copy of Resource Sheet 2
- Copies of Resource Sheet 2

Other Resources
- Highlighters
- Pencils

Introduction

Today we are going to search for new and interesting words and phrases in our reading, and then use them in our own writing.

Display the story 'Late for School' (Resource Sheet 2) and give the children their own copies as well.

Ask them to listen to the story while following the words.

Did you enjoy that story?

What made it interesting?

Are there any new and interesting words and phrases in this story that could help us in our own writing?

Model some of them by highlighting or underlining each word/phrase in the first paragraph; for example, 'tumbled' and 'wretched'.

Ask the children to highlight/underline the same words/phrases on their own copy of the story as you go through the first paragraph. Discuss why each was selected.

What does it mean?

What made it interesting?

Is it an action word or describing word?

Could I use it in my own writing? How?

Can you make up a sentence using this word/phrase?

Explain the activity. Remind them that if they are unsure of the meaning of the words, they should look them up in a dictionary.

Activity

AA 🎲 and MA 🎲
These children should find and highlight new and interesting words and phrases in the remainder of the text. They should then make up and write a new sentence for each interesting word or phrase they have found.

LA 🎲 & SEN
As a group, these children should also find and highlight new words and phrases in the remainder of the text. They should then orally place the new words in sentences which can be scribed by the adult. **With support.**

Key Vocabulary

words, phrases, interesting, writing, sentence, highlight, dictionary

---

Plenary

Share a selection of sentences from the different ability groups.

Which is the interesting word or phrase?

Is it an action word or describing word?

Tell the children that now they have found these interesting words and phrases, they should try to include them in their writing in the future.

Word Detective

Late For School

Rea was hurrying to fetch her school bag. But she wasn't looking where she was going. Whoops! She tumbled over the wretched pile of toys she had left in the hall. Mum had warned her not to leave them there. "Ouch!" yelped Rea. Her lip was trembling and she started to whimper.

Mum was in the kitchen baking muffins. When she heard the loud bang, she shot off full-speed into the hall to see what had happened. "What's the matter?" asked Mum. "I heard you shout."

"I was rushing. I tripped over and hurt my knee," howled Rea.

Mum gave Rea a big cuddle to make her feel better. Rea stopped sobbing and peered at her knee to see if there was a graze. "Why were you rushing?" asked Mum.

"Because I didn't want to be late for school," explained Rea, kneading her sore knee.

Mum grinned. "Oh Rea," she laughed. "It's Saturday. You don't go to school at the weekend!"

"Oops!" said Rea, giggling. Rea and Mum shared an oven-fresh muffin. Suddenly Rea's knee felt much better!

Perfect Postcard

Phonics Starter	Learning Objective	Introduction	Activity	Plenary

Learning Objective
- To recognise different graphemes for the 'ur' phoneme

Graphemes are letters.
Which different graphemes make the sound 'ur'?

Write the list below on the board.

ur – as in curl, church, turn
er – as in perfect, fern, verb
ir – as in bird, first, swirl
ear – as in heard, earn, pearl

Read each group of words out loud, asking the children to repeat them. Underline/ highlight (or ask a child to) the 'ur' phoneme in each.

If time:
Can you think of another word that contains that grapheme? Does it make the sound 'ur'?

Add their words to the lists. Repeat the process with the other words.

Learning Objective
- To plan and write a postcard using features of a non-chronological report

Success Criteria
- I can plan a postcard.
- I can write a postcard using my plan.

CD-ROM Resources
- PowerPoint file
- Slides 4 and 5 in the PowerPoint file or enlarged copies of Resource Sheets 1 and 2
- Copies of Activity Sheets 1 and 2

Other Resources
- Real postcards received to show the children
- Pens or pencils
- Crayons

Introduction

Today we are going to plan and write a postcard.

Where have you been that you might have sent a postcard from? Briefly discuss. Show any you might have.

Show and read the sample postcard (Resource Sheet 1). Then show the sample postcard plan (Resource Sheet 2) and explain how it was used to create the sample postcard.

If you were to receive a postcard, what would you expect to see on it?

Discuss:
- The name and address it is to be sent to
- A stamp
- Dear 'Your name'
- Introduction – where the person who sent it is/why they're writing/what they have been doing and how it felt – a lot of description to make it interesting
- What they are going to do next
- A sentence to finish, such as when they will see you again
- Who it is from

What do you use at the beginning of a sentence?
A capital letter.

What do you always put at the end of a sentence?
A full stop, question mark or exclamation mark.

Explain the activity.

Remind the children to use lots of describing words to make their postcard interesting.

Activity

Give each child a copy of Activity Sheets 1 and 2.

AA and MA
These children should individually complete the blank postcard plan, including information on how long it took to get there and one interesting fact about the place (which they may make up, if they wish). They should then use this plan to help them write their postcard.
Extension: On the other side, they could draw a picture of the place they are writing the postcard from, like on a real postcard.

LA & SEN
The children should do the same as above, but they may work as a group with adult support to scribe, if appropriate.
With support.
Extension: They could also draw a picture of the place they are writing the postcard from.

Key Vocabulary

introduction, description, sentence, capital letter, comma, full stop, plan, place, postcard, stamp, address, interesting

Plenary

Share a selection of postcards from each of the ability groups.

What interesting describing words have they used?

Would you like to visit that place?

Perfect Postcard

On the left ☑

On the right ☑

Dear (person's first name) _____

Stamp

Who is it to? _____

Their address _____

PostCARD

Introduction: Where you are and what it's like _____

What you have done _____

What you will do next _____

When you'll see them again _____

Who it is from _____

✱ Remember to add lots of description to make it interesting!

I can plan a postcard using these features. ☐

Making Toast

Phonics Starter	Learning Objective	Introduction	Activity	Plenary

Learning Objective
- To recognise the 'oa' grapheme within a word

Play 'Match the Grapheme'.

Display and read together all the words on this word list: goat, make, boat, leaf, loaf, light, load, moat, moon, croak, moan, green, toast, rain, toad, could, coat, goal, pain, soap

Who can find a word on the list that has a matching 'oa' grapheme?

Select children to read the word out loud, spell it out loud and then underline the 'oa' in the word in the list. They should then write it on the board while the rest of the class write the word in the air.

Learning Objective
- To write a set of instructions for making toast

Success Criteria
- I can write a set of instructions for making toast.

CD-ROM Resources
- PowerPoint file
- Slide 4 in the PowerPoint file or an enlarged version of Resource Sheet 1
- Slide 5 in the PowerPoint file or an enlarged version of Resource Sheet 2
- The differentiated Activity Sheets

Other Resources

For Phonics Starter
- A list for display of the words given (or Slide 1 in the PowerPoint file)

For the main lesson
- A sweatshirt
- Lined paper
- Scissors
- Glue
- Pencils/pens

Introduction

Today we are going to going to write a set of instructions for making toast.

What are instructions?

A list of short, clear sentences to tell you how to do something.

Why do instructions have to be exact?

So that what you do is done properly.

Show the instructions for putting on a sweatshirt (Resource Sheet 1) and allow time for the children to read them.

Explain that you are going to follow these instructions.

Read each line as you go. Deliberately put your head and arm in the wrong holes. Hopefully this will be an amusingly graphic example of why instructions must be very carefully thought out and worded.

Explain to the children that now they will look at how to write some instructions properly.

As a class, discuss the instructions for making a cup of tea.

Show the blank Instructions Flow Chart (Resource Sheet 2) and discuss what each box is for.

If we were going to write some instructions to make toast, what would we write on the flow chart?

Discuss what information would be in each box.

Explain the activity.

Activity

AA
These children should write a clear set of instructions to make toast, referring to the blank flow chart (Resource Sheet 2).

MA
These children should write a set of instructions to match the pictures on their Activity Sheet. This scaffold contains the pictures in the correct sequence, but the children have to write the instructions themselves.
Support as appropriate.

LA & SEN
These children should cut out the boxes of text on page 2 of their Activity Sheet. Each cut-out box should then be matched with the appropriate position and pictures on page 1 of their Activity Sheets. Once they have checked the order to make sure their text is in the correct position, the text boxes should be stuck down in place.
With support.

Key Vocabulary

instructions, list, clear, sentences, flow chart, toast, bread, toaster, knife, plate, butter

---

Plenary

Who can help me to write some instructions to put the sweatshirt on properly?

Select children to give you an instruction.

Select one child to put a sweatshirt on according to the instructions.

Making Toast: Instructions

How to

What you need

What to do	

I can write instructions to match the pictures. ☐

If I Could Be An Animal

Phonics Starter

Learning Objective
- To recognise different phonemes for the two-letter grapheme 'ea'

Draw a grid with three columns on the board. Write the word 'head' at the top of the first column and underline 'ea' in the word.

What is this word?

What sound does 'ea' have?
(Short e – /e/)

Can you think of other words that have the same phoneme (sound) for 'ea'?
(E.g. bread, deaf, feather.)

List them under 'head'.

Now write the word 'bead' at the top of the second column, and repeat the questions above. (The 'ea' phoneme is long e – /ee/ – as in deal, reach, stream.)

Finally, write the word 'great' at the top of the third column, and repeat the questions above. (The 'ea' phoneme is long a – /ai/ – as in break, breaker, steak, yea. Note that there are not many words in this category!)

Remind the children to consider all these different phoneme options for 'ea' in spelling and reading unfamiliar words.

Learning Objective

- To explore the effect of patterns of language and use them in the writing of poetry

Success Criteria

- I can write some new verses of a poem.

CD-ROM Resources

- PowerPoint file
- Slide 7 in the PowerPoint file or an enlarged copy of the Resource Sheet
- Copies of the differentiated Activity Sheets

Other Resources

- Pens or pencils

Introduction

Today we are going to write some of our own verses of a poem, carrying on the same pattern and style.

Display the poem 'If I Could Be An Animal' (Resource Sheet). Read it together.

What patterns do you notice?

Reread the poem. Elicit from the children that:
- each verse has three lines;
- the first line is always the same;
- the second line always begins with 'I would be a' and then has a describing word(s) followed by an animal;
- the third line always begins with an action word that ends in 'ing' and is appropriate to the animal;
- the third line contains describing words.

Explain to the children that writing is the same as being an artist – we 'paint a picture with words' to make our writing really interesting to read. The more detail we describe, the easier it is for the reader to see in their mind what we are describing.

Tell the children that their task is to write some of their own verses of the poem.

Reread the poem.

What other animals can you think of?
Suggest rabbit, hedgehog, worm and so on.

What action words can you think of to describe this animal?

What describing words can you think of that show how the animal behaves, looks or moves?

Mind-map the answers on the board in columns to help with vocabulary and ideas. Then model writing a verse.

Activity

AA 🗒
For each verse of their poem, these children should carefully copy the first line and the repeated portion of the second line, 'I would be a' and then continue the verse. They should write three to four verses, continuing the same pattern and style but adding a fourth line to each verse. For example, in the first verse, they could add the fourth line: 'Where the jellyfish swim and sway.' Point out that, as a result, the pattern of their poem will be different.

MA 🗒
These children should write two to three verses of the poem, continuing the same pattern and style, using the scaffold on their Activity Sheet, which has the first and part of the second lines written for them. This is to give them more time to compose their new lines.

LA 🗒 **& SEN**
These children should write two verses of the poem, continuing the same pattern and style, using the scaffold on their Activity Sheet, which contains the first line, then the first part of the second line for each verse. **Support.**

Key Vocabulary

poem, verse, pattern, style, adjectives, describing words, action words, verbs, animal

Plenary

Share some of the poetry, ensuring you include a selection from each of the ability groups.

Is the pattern the same?
Remember, it won't be for the 🗒 group.

Have they used a describing word before the name of the animal?

Have they used an action word ending in 'ing' to start their third line?

Are there lots of appropriate describing words?

If I Could Be An Animal

If I could be an animal,
I would be a playful dolphin
Dancing in the deep, turquoise sea.

If I could be an animal,
I would be a fierce tiger
Chasing an eland through the long grass.

If I could be an animal,
I would be a huge, grey elephant
Squirting water from my trunk like a fountain.

If I could be an animal,
I would be a sleepy cat
Snoozing in the warm afternoon sun.

A Poem About Me

Phonics Starter	Learning Objective	Introduction	Activity	Plenary
Learning Objective • To recognise different graphemes for the 'long e' phoneme Show the children the blank crossword and clues (Resource Sheet 1) Point to the first clue and read it out to the children. *What word are we looking for?* Choose a child to spell the word. If it is spelled correctly, ask them to write it in the correct place in the crossword. Tick the clue to show that it is solved. Repeat until the crossword is completed. **Answers:** Across: 1 scream; 3 eats; 6 key. down: 1 sleep, 2 me, 4 thief, 5 bee.	• To perform a poem appropriately, using suitable actions **Success Criteria** • I can perform a poem, using suitable actions. **CD-ROM Resources** • PowerPoint file • Slide 1 in the PowerPoint file or an enlarged copy of Resource Sheet 1 • Slide 4 in the PowerPoint file or an enlarged copy of Resource Sheet 2 • Copies of Resource Sheets 2 and 3	***Today we are going to practise and perform a poem and make up actions for each line.*** Display the poem 'Me' (Resource Sheet 2) and read it together. Discuss the pattern – A B C B. Read each line together and ask the children to repeat it several times. ***What action can we do to illustrate the line of the poem?*** If several actions are suggested, ask the children to vote on which they prefer. As a class, recite the line with the chosen action several times. Repeat this process until all of the lines of the first verse have an appropriate action. Send the children into their literacy groups and ask them to practise reciting the poem and the actions, so that they know it by heart (if possible) and can perform it and the actions smoothly. Remind the children that they all need to say the words at the same time. They also need to perform the actions in unison and in the correct place. Leave the copy of the poem on display so that the children can refer to it while practising.	**AA** These children, as a group, should develop additional actions for the second and third verses. They should then practise the poem for performance by heart. **MA** These children, as a group, should also develop additional actions for the second and third verses, but they can use a printed version (Resource Sheet 2) for a prompt as they practise the poem for performance. **LA & SEN** These children, as a group, should develop a performance of the poem using Resource Sheet 3, which offers action suggestions. **Support if appropriate.** **NB:** This lesson could be developed with the children writing their own verses or version of the poem. **Key Vocabulary** alliteration, sentence, action word, verb, capital letter, full stop, letter, same sound, phoneme, grapheme	The ability groups should take it in turns to perform the poem with the actions to the rest of the class. After each performance, ask the 'audience': ***What did you like about that performance?*** ***Which bit/line of the poem did you like best?*** Ask the performers: ***Did you find it easy to think up actions? Why/why not?*** ***What did you find most difficult about performing the poem as a group?***

A Poem About Me

Me

Two eyes, two ears,
One mouth and a nose.
Two hands and ten fingers,
I can count with those.

Two arms, two legs,
Two feet and ten toes.
I must take my shoes off
To count those.

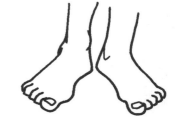

One head, one neck,
Two shoulders I own.
Two arms, two elbows,
A skeleton of bone.

BY CANDY ADLER AND KATIE COLLINS

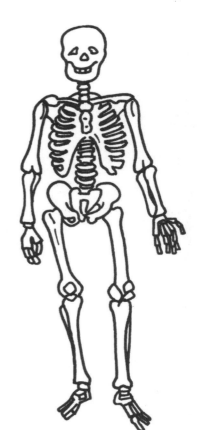

What If Cinderella... ?

Phonics Starter	Learning Objective	Introduction	Activity	Plenary
Learning Objective • To practise spelling high-frequency words Play the 'Speed Read' game. Explain to the children that you are going to show them a list of words and they are to read them as a group. Use a timer to time how long it takes the class to read them all. *Can you do it again, beating your first time?* **CD-ROM Resources** • PowerPoint file • Slide 4 in the PowerPoint file or an enlarged copy of the Activity Sheet • Copies of the Activity Sheet **Other Resources** • Paper • Pens or pencils	• To explore familiar themes and characters through improvisation and role-play: alternative endings to Cinderella **Success Criteria** • I can role-play alternative endings to the story of Cinderella. The words are: **little** **play** **what** **they** **have** **down** **back** **off**	*Today we are going to role-play alternative endings to the story of Cinderella.* *What does the word 'alternative' mean?* Different. *Who can remind us of the story of Cinderella?* Select children from different ability groups to each give a synopsis of part of the story. Explain that they are now going to act out different endings to the story. *Now, we all know that Cinderella marries the Prince and lives happily ever after, but what if:* Display and read the questions from the 'Alternative Endings' list on the Activity Sheet. Explain to the children that they are going to go into groups and discuss which question they want to explore. There are two blank spaces in case the group wants to think of their own 'What if...' questions.	**ALL ABILITY GROUPS** The children should work as a group, discussing which question they want to answer in order to find an alternative story ending. They should then role-play different aspects of the story until they agree on a suitable storyline. One child should be elected as scribe to jot down the agreed ending. **AA & MA** These children should devise their own ending to act out, bullet-pointing the different suggestions. **Provide support for children if appropriate.** **LA & SEN** An adult should act as scribe to jot down bullet points for the agreed ending. **With support.** **NB** The lesson could culminate in the groups using the jotted bullet points to write out their alternative ending in full. **Key Vocabulary** alternative ending, story, traditional, retell, role-play, act out, storyline, elect, scribe	An elected spokesperson from each group should feed back their group's alternative story ending. *Would that work?* *What sort of traditional story language could you use?* **NB**: If the children have gone on to write the story ending in full, use the following questions: *Have they used the traditional story language?* *Is it interesting?* *Have they used lots of strong words and description?*

What If Cinderella... ?

Alternative Endings

Marry you? No way!

✱ Consider these alternative endings or write your own.

- What if Cinderella decided that she didn't want to marry the prince?

- What if Cinderella got lost on her way to the ball? How would she meet the Prince? Would she meet someone else?

- What if Cinderella didn't leave the ball just before midnight?

- What if Cinderella did not leave a glass slipper behind?

- What if one of the ugly step-sisters' foot fit in the slipper first?

- What if _____

  _____

- What if _____

  _____

I can role-play alternative endings to the story of Cinderella. ☐

Partner Patterns — Literacy

Phonics Starter	Learning Objective	Introduction	Activity	Plenary

Phonics Starter

Learning Objective
- To recognise alternative phonemes for the two-letter grapheme 'ow'

Display the following list of words on the board:

low	cow
now	show
yellow	frown
towel	blow

What do all these words have in common?

The two-letter grapheme 'ow'.

Does the two-letter grapheme 'ow' make the same sound in all the words?

What other words contain 'ow'?

Which group do they belong in?

Add them to the lists.

As a whole class sort them into two groups – 'ow' as in low and 'ow' as in cow.

Learning Objective
- To listen to and follow instructions accurately

Success Criteria
- I can take turns to give, listen and follow instructions.

CD-ROM Resources
- PowerPoint file
- Copies of the Resource Sheet

Other Resources
- Whiteboards and pens
- Pre-prepared drawing of a pattern that is made up of a square, an arrow and a circle

---

Introduction

Today we are going to concentrate on listening carefully to a partner giving instructions and draw the patterns they describe.

Give out whiteboards and pens.

Tell the children to listen carefully to your instructions. They are to draw exactly what you tell them to. Explain that it is important that they do not copy someone else's work – that person may be wrong.

- *Draw a square*
- *Draw an arrow*
- *Draw a circle*

Ask the children to show you their patterns – they should be quite varied.

Show them the pattern you have just described.

How could I have made the instructions clearer?

Select a child to suggest clearer instructions and draw their shape on the board. For example:

- *Draw an arrow in the middle of the board, pointing to the right.*
- *Draw a circle touching the pointed end.*
- *Draw a square touching the other end.*

Compare this latest picture with the ones drawn before.

Look at the language used and discuss.

What words might we need to describe the patterns? (See Key Vocabulary.) Point out that most of these are words we use in maths. Write them on the board.

Explain the activity.

Activity

IN PAIRS WITHIN ABILITY GROUPS

Using copies of the Resource Sheet, cut out relevant shape patterns for each pair – note they are differentiated for different abilities. Hand them one at a time to the child who is to describe the shape, ensuring their partner does not see it.

The children should sit back-to-back, with those giving the instructions sitting so that they can see the vocabulary list on the board.

The first child should quietly describe the pattern step-by-step to their partner. The partner should try to follow the instructions to replicate the described pattern on their whiteboard.

When they have finished, the children should sit silently while the other pairs finish. Ask everyone to compare their patterns. Discuss what was the same, what went wrong and how the language could have been improved.

(If you prefer, as they finish let the pairs compare patterns, come to you for approval, then issue a new one.)

The pairs change places and repeat the activity with their new shape.

Key Vocabulary

position, right, left, on top, above, below, under, around, touching, next to, inside, pointed end, other end, circle, square, shape, pentagon, hexagon, arrow

---

Plenary

Select a child to use their pattern and instruct you to draw it.

Have they used mathematical directional and positional language?

Were the instructions given in a clear voice?

Were the instructions precise?

How could they have improved on the instructions?

If time, repeat with another child to speak and a second to follow the instructions.

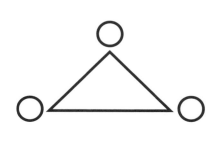

Partner Patterns

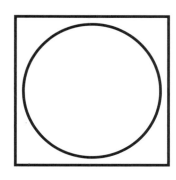 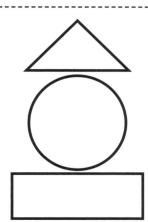

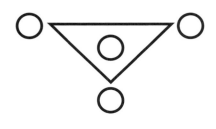 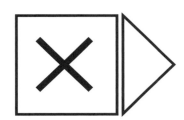 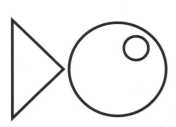

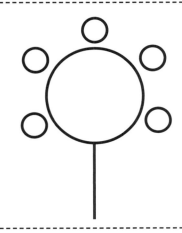 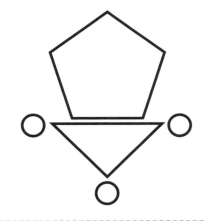 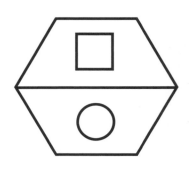

Phonics Starter	Learning Objective	Introduction	Activity	Plenary

Learning Objective
- To recognise that some phonemes are represented by more than one grapheme

Play the 'Odd One Out' game.

Write a list of three words on the board.

Can you find the odd one out?

All of the words have the same two-letter grapheme. Two words have the same phoneme and one word has a different phoneme.

Repeat this with other groups of words.

Examples:

1. boot, tool, **look**
2. **head**, each, heal
3. **thief**, cried, pie
4. crown, **snow**, town
5. rain, pain, **said**
6. **easy**, bread, thread
7. **brown**, own, grow
8. **field**, die, tried

Learning Objective
- To explore a character's point of view through role-play

Success Criteria
- I can explore a character's point of view through role-play.

CD-ROM Resources
- PowerPoint file
- Slide 6 in the PowerPoint file or an enlarged copy of the Resource Sheet

Other Resources
- A2 sheets of paper
- Pencils or pens

Introduction

Today we are going to think about the story of Little Red Riding Hood and role-play the story from some of the characters' points of view.

What are the main parts of the story of Little Red Riding Hood?

Grandma not well, Little Red Riding Hood takes food to her, Big Bad Wolf gets there first and eats Grandma and then pretends to be her, Wolf ends up eating Little Red Riding Hood and the woodcutter cuts the wolf open to free Little Red Riding Hood and Grandma.

Tell the children they are going to think about the points of view of the different characters as the story develops: Little Red Riding Hood, Wolf, Woodcutter, Grandma.

What does 'point of view' mean? How someone feels about something.

To demonstrate, use Red Riding Hood's parents as an example. Why are they sending Red Riding Hood to take food to Grandma instead of going themselves? How do they feel now that Red Riding Hood is late home? Did they know she would walk through the wood? Did they know there was a wolf there?

Display the Resource Sheet. Model writing a few notes on the mind-map of the parents' points of view, as an example of what you expect from the children.

What else might the parents be feeling or thinking?

Fill in some or all of the speech bubbles.

Sort the children into mixed ability groups and allocate them a character. Give them an A2 sheet of paper. A high ability child in each group should be the scribe.

Explain the activity.

Activity

IN MIXED ABILITY GROUPS

The scribe for each group should write the names of the group members on the back of the sheet and label the front with the character they are mind-mapping.

Little Red Riding Hood
The Wolf
The Woodcutter
Grandma

In their groups, the children should role-play the story. They should stop at each event to discuss what has just happened from their character's point of view: how the character felt, what they thought and what made them do what they did. They must remember to value the opinions of each group member. The scribe should make notes on every point made.

The teacher and support staff should circulate, helping with the note-making.

Finally, the groups should select a spokesperson to feed back their work to the class in the plenary session.

NB: This lesson can be extended by using the mind-maps as notes to rewrite the original story, but from their character's point of view.

Key Vocabulary

point of view, role-play, feelings, motivation, discuss, spokesperson, feedback, value, opinion, character

Plenary

Select one group's spokesperson to feed back to the class.

Ask the class:

Do you agree with this group that this is how the character felt?

Why? Why not?

Do you think the character would feel differently? How?

Ask the scribe to add any valid information to their mind-map.

Repeat this for each group's character.

How Did They Feel?

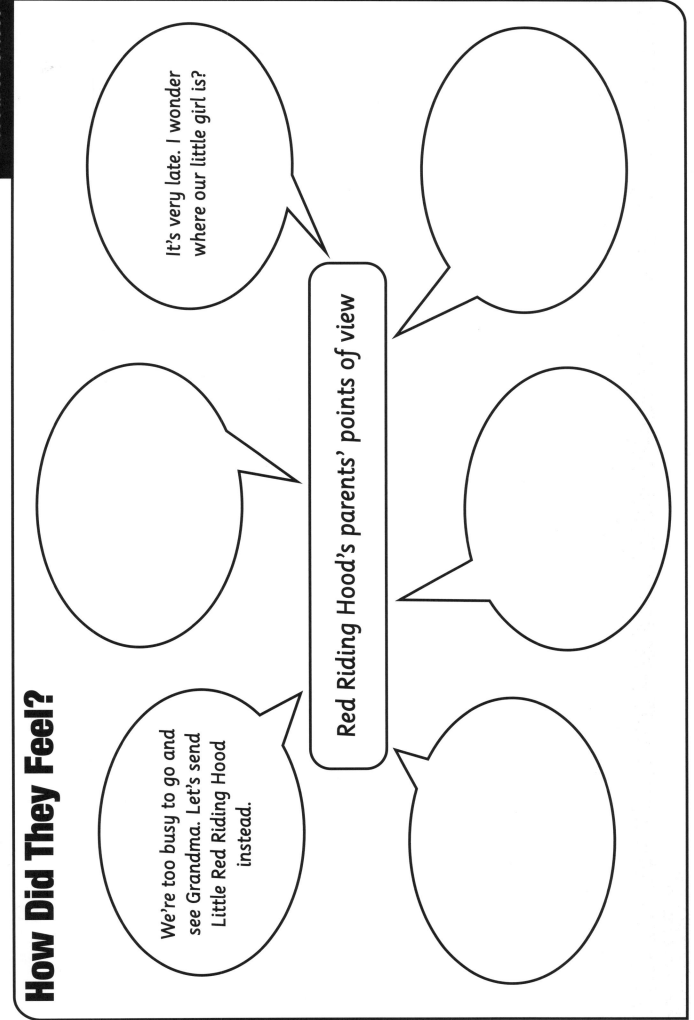

It's very late. I wonder where our little girl is?

We're too busy to go and see Grandma. Let's send Little Red Riding Hood instead.

Red Riding Hood's parents' points of view

The Lonely Dolphin

Phonics Starter	Learning Objective	Introduction	Activity	Plenary

Learning Objective
- To recognise different graphemes for the 'long i' phoneme.

Show the list of words below.

butterfly   cries   light   wild
child   night   try   tied   mind
might   pry   fried   sight   I
spied   my   right   find   why
relied   blind   find   fry   dry
tried   kind   dried   delight
behind   fight   lie   sky
remind   pie   reply

Explain that they all have a 'long i' sound, but don't always have the same letters making up that sound.

Can you highlight the letter/letters that indicate the 'long i' sound?

Ask the children to sort the words according to the graphemes making the long 'i' sound.

Can you think of another word that has a 'long i' sound?

Can you spell it?

Either you or individual children should write any new words found on the board.

Learning Objective
- To explore the effects of language patterns and repeated words and phrases

Success Criteria
- I can explore the effects of language patterns and repeated words and phrases.
- I can continue a story, using the same pattern.

CD-ROM Resources
- PowerPoint file
- Slides 4 and 5 in the PowerPoint file or an enlarged copy of the Resource Sheet (both pages 1 and 2)
- Copies of the Activity Sheet

Other Resources

For Phonics Starter
- A list for display of the words given (or Slide 1 in the PowerPoint file)
- Pens or pencils
- Lined paper

Today we are going to continue a story using a repeating pattern.

Display the story 'The Lonely Dolphin' (Resource Sheet pages 1 and 2) and read it together.

What happened in the story?

What do you notice about the language of the story when Dawnie the dolphin begins to look for a new friend?
Discuss the repeated language pattern.

Can you think of an animal that does not live in water? Where does it live?
List some of the children's suggestions on the board.

Now can you think of an animal that does live in water?
List these on the board.

Tell the children that they are going to write some new bits of the story, using the same repeated language, about the dolphin meeting new friends and asking them to come and live with her.

Remember: the last animal will swim off with her.

NB: This lesson can be extended or adapted to make a class book including pictures. It could also be used as the topic for a role-play session.

AA
Independently, these children should make up a story (on lined paper) with a repeated language pattern similar to that on page 2 of the story. It should contain at least two animals that can't live in water, and one that can.

MA
Independently, on lined paper, these children should use the same wording as the story, but write their own versions. They should write the last three lines of the story in their own words. They should write about at least two animals that can't live in water and one that can.

LA & SEN
Independently, these children should use the scaffold on the Activity Sheet. They should add their own animals and where they live. Remind them that the first animals they choose should not be able to live in water. Then, for the last bit, they should write about an animal that can live in the sea.
Supported.

NB: Early Year 1 children may need to use the Sheet and work in either groups or pairs, depending on their ability.

Extension (for all groups):
The children can illustrate each section of patterned language with a picture of the creature that Dawnie the dolphin met.

Key Vocabulary

story, ending, repeating, pattern, language

Share some of the verses from each ability group.

When you have heard a group story, ask:

Did their story have a repeated pattern similar to the one in the original story?

What lines were repeated?

Which animals did they choose? Why?

Listen to some of the stories produced by the group.

The Lonely Dolphin

"I'm a dolphin and I love to play!
You love to play too.
Will you come and live with me in the sea?"
"No, I'm a _____.
I live in _____.
I can't live in the water."

"I'm a dolphin and I love to play.
You love to play too.
Will you come and live with me in the sea?"
"No, I'm a _____.
I live in _____.
I can't live in the water."

"I'm a dolphin and I love to play.
You love to play too.
Will you come and live with me in the sea?"
"No, I'm a _____.
I live in _____.
I can't live in the water."

"I'm a dolphin and I love to play.
You love to play too.
Will you come and live with me in the sea?"
"Yes, I will."
So Dawnie Dolphin swam off
To play with her new friend,
_____.

And she was no longer lonely!

I can continue a story using the same pattern. ☐

What Fruit Or Vegetable Am I?

Learning Objective

- To understand that eating the right types and amounts of food help humans to keep healthy

Success Criteria

- I can understand that my body needs fruits and vegetables to be healthy.
- I can recognise common fruits and vegetables.

CD-ROM Resources

- PowerPoint file
- Slide 3 in the PowerPoint file or an enlarged copy of Resource Sheet 1
- Slide 5 in the PowerPoint file or an enlarged copy of Resource Sheet 2
- Copies of the differentiated Activity Sheets

Other Resources

- Scissors
- Glue
- A4 blank paper
- Coloured pencils

Introduction

Today we are going to look at some different fruits and vegetables that help to keep us healthy. We are going to see if we can identify the fruits and vegetables, and match their descriptions to the pictures.

What do we need to keep us healthy?
Food, water, air, sleep and exercise.

Why do we need food?
To give us energy (so that we are not too tired to do anything), to help us to grow and to keep us healthy.

What foods do our bodies need to be healthy?
Show the 'Healthy Portions Plate' (Resource Sheet 1). Discuss the contents of each portion.

Why do you think that the food groups are all different sizes?
Explain that, for a balanced diet and to be really healthy, we need to eat these amounts of each group.

Why do we need to eat fruit and vegetables?
Vitamins and minerals found in them are an essential (important) part of our diets to help us keep healthy, grow and live longer.

Do you know of any fruits or vegetables that need cooking?
Discuss the fact that fresh, frozen, tinned and juiced fruits are all good for us.

As a whole class, go through the list of fruit and vegetables (Resource Sheet 2). Uncover the first picture and see if anyone can guess what it is, then uncover its name and description. Repeat this, working down through the list.

What do you think might happen to you if you don't eat a variety of foods?
You won't grow so well and won't be able to fight off infections so easily.

Explain the activity.

Activity

AA
These children should write down on their sheet whether the picture is of a fruit or vegetable, and then write a short description to match each of them.

MA
These children should read each description, match a name to it using the word bank, and then draw a line to match the picture to their description.

LA & SEN
In pairs, these children should cut out the pictures of fruits and vegetables, names and descriptions and reassemble them to make a chart showing the correct information.
Support if required.

Extension: For all children. Think of another fruit or vegetable – real or imaginary. Draw and label it and make up your description.

Key Vocabulary

growth, health/y, diet, variety, vegetables, fruits, food groups, balanced, eat, infections, illnesses

Plenary

Display Resource Sheet 2 again.

What fruit/vegetable is this?

Are there any of these fruits or vegetables that you haven't seen before?

Are there any that you haven't eaten before?

How many do you eat a day?

Can you think of any ways to include more?
For example, having salad in sandwiches and fruit for dessert at lunchtime.

What else can we do to help keep our bodies healthy?
Drink water (rather than pop), and get plenty of fresh air, sleep and exercise.

What Fruit or Vegetable Am I?

✳ Read each description and decide which name it matches, using the word bank below. Write the name.

✳ Then match the picture to the name by drawing a line.

| courgette kiwi leek aubergine raspberry |
| green bean pepper melon |

	_ _ _ _ _ I am usually big and round. I can be yellow, white, green or a browny colour. Inside I have lots of pips. My flesh can be yellow, orange or red. I am juicy.
	_ _ _ _ I am long and thin, white at the bottom and green at the top. I am delicious cut up and served with cheese sauce. I am the national emblem of Wales.
	_ _ _ _ _ _ _ _ _ I am very small, round and red. I have a similar name to another summer fruit that is usually eaten with cream.
	_ _ _ _ _ _ _ _ _ I look like a small cucumber. I am usually sliced and cooked, but sometimes I'm stuffed with other food, such as rice or peppers, and then cooked.
	_ _ _ _ _ _ _ _ _ I am a deep purple colour, large and sausage shaped. In some countries I am called an egg plant. I am a fruit but people use me as a vegetable.
	_ _ _ _ _ _ _ _ _ _ _ Gardeners like to grow me and usually give me poles to grow on. I am green, long and thin. You can cook me whole or cut me into smaller pieces.
	_ _ _ _ I am small and oval. I have a brown, furry skin but inside I am green with a black star pattern. I am delicious eaten sliced or cut in half and scooped out with a spoon.
	_ _ _ _ _ _ I can be red, yellow, orange and green, and am sometimes described as 'bell' shaped. You can eat me raw or cooked.

I can recognise fruits and vegetables in their raw state. ☐

Learning Objective	Introduction	Activity	Plenary
• To recognise similarities and differences between themselves and others through observations and measurements	*Today we are going to collect data (information) to answer the question: 'Are our elbows all the same size?' To do this we need to measure each other's elbows and make a graph to represent the data (show the information).*	**IN ABILITY GROUPS** Each child should have their own data table (from Activity Sheet 4) and appropriate Activity Sheet. There should be six children in a group. Taking it in turns, one child should measure the circumference of another child's elbow and another child should check the measurement. The name of the child measured should be written into the table and the measurement in the box next to it. The children should record individually. **All measurements should be to the nearest cm.** The second child should then measure someone, and so on, until all the children in their group have been measured.	Show an enlarged copy of the grid on Activity Sheet 5. Ask each group in turn how many in that group have elbows that measure a specific size, starting with 18cm. Make a note of the number. Add up the number of children altogether that have that size and complete the grid accordingly as a block graph. Do this for each cm measurement up to 28cm, entering the information on the graph as you total the numbers.
Success Criteria	Explain to the children that every single person is slightly different from everybody else. We are all unique. Say that we are only looking at characteristics (things about us) that we are born with or that develop (grow), such as eye colour or length of hair, not the things that we wear or own.		
• I can measure elbows and use the data to make a block graph.	*What little differences can you think of?* Eye shape, foot size, hand span, freckles, height and so on.	**AA** 🖂 Individually, these children should agree and write a title for their research. They should then label and complete the block graph, by writing in the names of the children in their group and colouring the squares to represent the number of cm their elbows measured. For example, if a child's elbow measures 20cm, the children should colour in the 18, 19 and 20 spaces above the child's name.	Explain to the class that they are now going to use the graph to answer some questions. *Are everyone's elbows the same size?* *How do you know?*
CD-ROM Resources	Explain to the children that they are going to answer the question 'Are our elbows all the same size?'		*How many cm are most children's elbows?*
• PowerPoint file • Copies of Activity Sheet 4 (Data Tables), cut up • Copies of the differentiated Activity Sheets (one per child) • Slide 7 in the PowerPoint file or an enlarged copy of Activity Sheet 5	*Does anyone know another name for the elbow?* Funny bone. *It certainly isn't funny when you hit it because it hurts very much, so why is it called a funny bone?* Explain that the elbow is at the bottom of the upper arm, which, in medical terms, is called the humerus. Write 'humerus' on the board. This, of course, sounds like 'humorous', which means funny or amusing, a sort of joke (also, sense of humour). Write 'humorous' on the board to show the difference in spelling.	**MA** 🖂 Individually, these children should label the axes and complete the block graph, by writing in the names of the children in their group and colouring the squares to represent the number of cm their elbows measured, as for the 🖂 group.	*How many cm do the fewest children measure?*
Other Resources	Model, with the help of a child, measuring around an elbow with the elbow bent to 90°. Make sure you measure the complete circle. Explain the activity.	**LA** 🖂 **& SEN** These children should work in pairs or as a group, whichever is appropriate, but recording individually. They should complete the block graph, by writing in the names of the children in their group and colouring the squares to represent the number of cm their elbows measured, as for the 🖂 group. **Supported.**	
• Measuring tapes or strips of wool or string long enough to measure the circumference of children's elbows • Rulers • Pencils	Model filling in the data table and completing a block graph using one square to represent each centimetre.	**Key Vocabulary** **collect data, differences, arm, elbow, data table, block graph, wider, narrower, measure, interpret, compare**	

Funny Bones

Are our elbows all the same size?

Number of centimetres measured						
27						
26						
25						
24						
23						
22						
21						
20						
19						
18						

Names of children measured

I can measure elbows **b**ond use the data to make a block graph. ☐

Memory Blanket

Learning Objective	Introduction	Activity	Plenary
• To record, by drawing, a special event or occasion or achievement from first-hand experience	*Today we are going to search our memories to think of a really special time in our lives and then draw it really carefully. We will then stick everyone's together to make a memory blanket.* Ask the children to sit in a circle with the same rules as circle time. Select an object to hand round. No one is to speak unless they are holding the object. The children can pass if they really can't think of an answer to the question and you can go back to them. Explain that people often keep photographs or keepsakes to remind them of special events in their lives.	Individually, the children should draw a scene of their special achievement or an event of which they have really fond memories. It is to be a 'photograph' of the time, so should have lots of detail and cover the whole page. They should leave enough space above the line to write a sentence. The teacher and other adult/s should circulate and scribe, writing on the children's whiteboards for them to label their work. **Extension:** The children could colour in the 'photo frame'.	Share as much of the children's work as possible. *Does this one have lots of little details, like a photograph does?* *Do you think it will remind you of your achievement or special occasion?* *How do you think you could improve it?* Sticky tape the sheets together to make the memory blanket. If there are not sufficient memories to make a rectangle or square, you could add a class label and an explanation. Alternatively, mount each sheet on coloured paper or stick it onto different coloured fabric, so that it looks like a colourful patchwork quilt. Explain to the children that quilting was an early American pastime. Handmade quilts were a common wedding gift for young couples. Sometimes the quilts were made to reflect a picture of someone's life, often including swatches of material from memorable events such as pieces of a wedding gown or a child's baptismal garment.
Success Criteria • I can draw a picture of a special occasion or achievement with lots of detail, like in a photograph.	*What is a keepsake?* Describe a few events of which you have kept photographs and keepsakes. For example, "I have photographs of my graduation from university. I have also kept a photo of my son when he was born, a lock of my son's hair and his first pair of shoes."		
CD-ROM Resources • PowerPoint file • Slide 4 in the PowerPoint file or an enlarged copy of the Activity Sheet • Copies of the Activity Sheet	*Have you kept any keepsakes to remind you of a special event in your life?* Pass the object round for a minute or so. *What is a special occasion or achievement?* For example, when a sibling was born; grandparents' wedding anniversary; a family wedding; very first day at school; first time achievements, such as rode a bike without stabilisers.		
Other Resources • Pencils • Coloured pencils • Whiteboards and pens	*Can you think of a very special occasion or achievement in your life that you have fond memories of – one that makes you smile whenever you think about it, even after all this time?* Give the children a couple of minutes to think about it and then use the object to work round the circle to check that everyone has an idea and that it is suitable to use for the memory blanket. Show the children the Activity Sheet they will be working on. Tell them to ask themselves: *If I picture the time in my mind, what can I see? What is around me? Who is there? What are we wearing? What colours can I see? What is the weather like?*	**Key Vocabulary** **draw, label, photograph, scene, picture in your mind, memory, blanket, keepsake, occasion, achievement, detailed**	

Memory Blanket

Wrap It Up!

Learning Objective

- To explore visual elements: pattern and colour

Success Criteria

- I can design wrapping paper for a special occasion and special person, using a repeated pattern.

CD-ROM Resources

- PowerPoint file
- Slides 4, 5 and 6 in the PowerPoint file or an enlarged copy of the Resource Sheet
- Copies of the Activity Sheet

Other Resources

- Samples of wrapping paper
- Paper
- Pens, pencils
- Colouring materials

Introduction

Today we are going to design wrapping paper for a special occasion and person, using patterns involving shapes, objects and colours.

What special occasions can you think of where we buy presents for other people? Birthday, Christmas, anniversary, Valentine's Day, new baby, wedding.

Why do you think we might wrap the presents we buy? Surprise element, pleasure in unwrapping it.

Ask the children to think about a present they have received. *What colour was the wrapping paper? Was it a pattern or pictures? Can you describe it?*

Explain that wrapping paper is designed for many different people and special occasions in a variety of colours, patterns and pictures to reflect the occasion.

Show the children the Resource Sheet and point to the paper with hearts and champagne glasses. *What occasion might this be to celebrate?* Wedding.

What are the clues that made you think that? Various wedding symbols – rings, hearts, champagne.

Point to the football paper.
Who do you think would like a present wrapped in this paper? Someone who loves football.

Point to the new baby paper.
Who do you think it might be designed for? Why?
New girl baby – pink; baby symbols: bottle, rattle, pram, dummy, stork, pram.

Point to the balloons paper.
What occasion would this be suitable for? Who for?
Any celebration/any gender/any age – birthday, graduation, anniversary, retirement.

Point to the Christmas paper.
What occasion would this be suitable for? How can you tell?
Christmas; red and green traditional Christmas colours, tree-shaped pattern. Discuss the use of repeated pattern and colour.

Point out that whether a pattern or pictures are used, they are all presented in a repeated pattern.

Explain the activity.

Activity

ALL ABILITY GROUPS

Individually, the children should think of a special occasion and person to design wrapping paper for, and write them on the Activity Sheet.

Design:
The children should think about what materials they might use for their design; for example:

- drawing on paper, cutting out the pictures, patterns or shapes and sticking them onto paper to give a textured look;
- using fabric or foil instead of paper.

They should:

- decide whether to draw appropriate pictures, use shapes or patterns;
- consider how their objects are to be repeated;
- consider what colours they could use;
- complete three separate designs for the same occasion and person;
- select the design they prefer and write the number of this design on the sheet in the space provided;
- explain the reason for their choice in the space provided.

LA & SEN

Support these children in the completion of the written part of the design and with the formulation of their ideas, if appropriate.

Key Vocabulary

special occasion, celebrate, suitable, wrapping paper, design, pattern, repeated, colour, materials

Plenary

Select some children to show the class their designs, covering the top of the sheet where it describes the occasion and person designed for.

What occasion do you think this wrapping paper was designed for?

What clues make you think that?

Who do you think it might have been designed for?

Why?

Wrap It Up!

My wrapping paper design

What occasion is it for? _____

Who is it for? _____

Materials I will use _____

_____

My pattern ideas:

```
┌─────────────────────────────────────────┐
│ 1                                         │
│                                           │
│                                           │
│                                           │
│                                           │
└─────────────────────────────────────────┘
```

```
┌─────────────────────────────────────────┐
│ 2                                         │
│                                           │
│                                           │
│                                           │
│                                           │
└─────────────────────────────────────────┘
```

```
┌─────────────────────────────────────────┐
│ 3                                         │
│                                           │
│                                           │
│                                           │
│                                           │
└─────────────────────────────────────────┘
```

I have chosen pattern ___ because _____

I can design wrapping paper for a special occasion and special person, using a repeated pattern. ☐

Where in the World?

Learning Objective	Introduction	Activity	Plenary
• To recognise how places are linked to other places in the world (for example, food from other countries)	**Today we are going to find out where some of the food that we eat comes from.**

Tell the children that when you were unpacking the shopping and putting it away the other day, you began to wonder where it all came from in the first place. Explain that some of the ingredients in our food do not come from this country.

How do you think food might be brought to this country (what transport might bring it)?
Aeroplane, boat, lorry, train.

Show the world map on Resource Sheet 1.
Who can show us on this map where we live?

Who can tell me what pasta is? (For example, spaghetti and noodles.)

Pasta is made from durum wheat. Can someone name a country that wheat for pasta comes from?

Reveal the top part of Resource Sheet 2.
Many people think it comes from Italy in Europe because that's where pasta is eaten at many mealtimes. There are also Italian pasta restaurants here, but most wheat for pasta comes from other countries. One of those is Canada in North America.

Who can show us where Europe and North America are on the map? Who can find Italy and Canada?

Now, what foods can you think of that contain sugar?
Sugar is in lots of things: sweets, jam, chocolate, cakes, biscuits.

Reveal the second part of Resource Sheet 2.
Did you know that it is also hidden in things like bread, tinned vegetables and fruits? There are two basic types of sugar: sugar beet, a lot of which is grown in the UK, and sugar cane, which comes from places like the islands of Jamaica and Barbados in the Caribbean, the island of Fiji in the South Pacific Ocean, and the island of Mauritius in the Indian Ocean.
Point to these places on the world map. Choose a child to mark them with a coloured pen.

Explain the activity. | **IN LITERACY ABILITY GROUPS**

Leave on display an atlas or the world map for guidance.

AA 🁫

These children should be given a list containing six pictures and names of foods (🁫 from Resource Sheet 3), and Activity Sheet 🁰 with a map of the world on which the relevant countries are marked only with a dot. The Activity Sheet also contains six boxes labelled with six parts of the world. They should work in pairs to decide, by a process of trial and error, which product fits which box. They should then write the name of the product in the box and draw a line from the box to the correct place on the map.

MA 🁰

These children have the same task as the AA children, but the list of foods they are given (🁱 from Resource Sheet 3) to match to the world map (Activity Sheet 🁰) includes the names of the places where the food comes from. They should work in pairs to draw the food in the correct boxes and draw a line to the correct place on the map.

LA 🁯 **& SEN**

These children have the same task as the other children but both their Activity Sheet (🁯) and list of foods (🁯 from Resource Sheet 3) include the name of the place where the food comes from. They should work in pairs to draw the food in the boxes and draw lines to the correct places on the map.
Support. | **Can you name all the different countries we have mentioned outside our country?**
Write them on the board.

Were you surprised to find that the products or foods actually came from around the world?

Which foods surprised you the most?

Next time you go shopping, look on the back of the packet of food, or ask whoever you go with if they can read it for you, to see which country it comes from.

Remind the children that the countries marked on their maps are only some of the places where the different foods come from. |
| **Success Criteria**
• I can find some of the countries that our food comes from on a world map. | | | |
| **CD-ROM Resources**
• PowerPoint file
• Slide 4 in the PowerPoint file or an enlarged copy of Resource Sheet 1
• Slide 7 in the PowerPoint file or an enlarged copy of Resource Sheet 2
• Copies of differentiated Resource Sheet 3
• A3 copies of the differentiated Activity Sheets | | | |
| **Other Resources**
• Atlases
• Writing and colouring materials | | **Key Vocabulary**

comes from, world, country, continent, travel, transport, England, Scotland, Wales, Ireland, grown, produce, ingredient | |

Where in the World?

North America

France

China

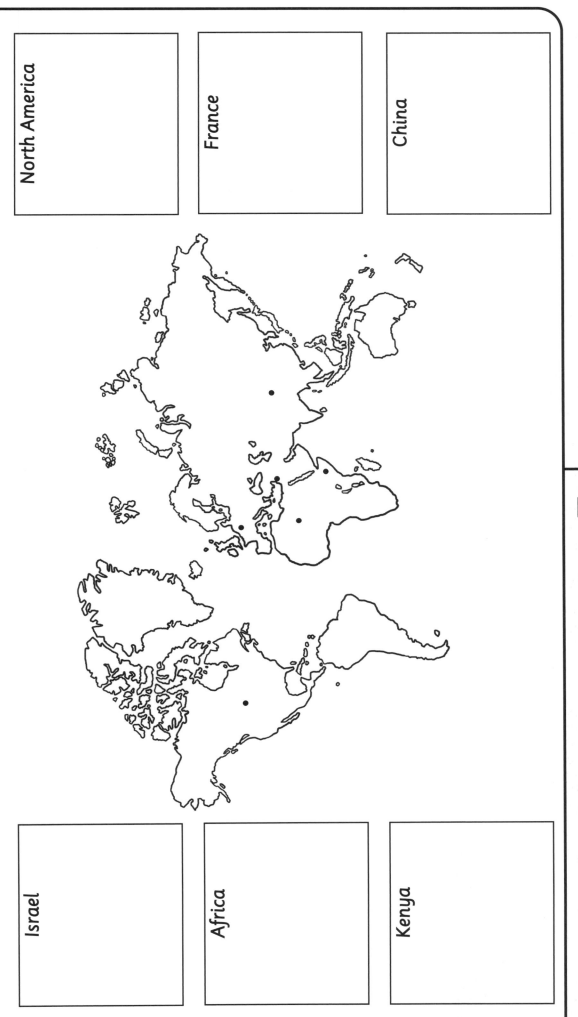

Israel

Africa

Kenya

I can find some of the countries that our food comes from on a world map. ☐

Can You Recycle?

Learning Objective

- To recognise how the environment may be improved and sustained by recycling

Success Criteria

- I can investigate what happens to a drink can when it is recycled.

CD-ROM Resources

- PowerPoint file
- Slide 5 in the PowerPoint file or an enlarged copy of Resource Sheet 1
- Copies of the differentiated Activity Sheets
- Copies of Resource Sheet 2

Other Resources

- Scissors
- Glue
- Pencils
- Coloured pencils

Introduction

Today we are going to discuss recycling waste, and then investigate what happens to the fizzy drink and baked beans can, first when we throw it away, and then when we recycle it.

What does 'recycling' mean? To re-use something.
What does 'waste' mean? Rubbish – things we throw away.

What happens to waste that is not recycled?
It is collected up in big lorries that compact (squash) it so that more can be thrown in the back. It is then driven to the tip, where it is tipped out into huge piles. It is then buried in a gigantic hole which is filled in again. This is called landfill. The rubbish stays there for a very long time, some of it perhaps for ever.

What things can we recycle from home?
Discuss the obvious things, such as cans, plastic drink bottles and paper. Explain that only a few years ago, people didn't throw things away when they were broken and then buy new ones, such as televisions and washing machines. They used to pay someone to repair them. They also used to reuse glass bottles by refilling them. Now local councils provide recycling boxes and centres.

What things that we don't use anymore, but that aren't broken, can we recycle instead of throw away?
Clothes that we have grown out of, toys, furniture, plates, ornaments – these can all go to charity shops. They are then sold to someone else and the charity makes money to help people in need.

What happens to the baked beans and drink cans that we recycle?
Display Resource Sheet 1. Talk through the different stages:
1. Empty the drink can.
2. Put it into recycling box or bank.
3. It is collected and taken to be sorted and compacted.
4. It is transported to factories to be melted and rolled into sheets and coils.
5. It is made into bikes, paperclips, cars, bridges, more drinks cans and lots of other things.

Explain the activity.

Activity

The children should work in pairs, but record individually. Leave Resource Sheet 1 on display for their information.

AA
These children should complete their Activity Sheet in writing, giving the five stages of recycling cans in the correct order, together with brief details. Then, in the box at the bottom of the sheet, they should draw and label some products that are made from recycled cans.

MA
These children should be given a set of individual labels cut out from Resource Sheet 2. They should stick them into the five stages of recycling cans in the correct order. Next, they should complete all six example boxes by drawing and labelling the products that are made from recycled cans, using the word bank to help them. They should work out for themselves that the drink can goes in the top left box with the up arrow.

LA
As for **MA** except that the product labels can be cut and pasted.

SEN
These children should read the labels in the five stages of recycling cans in the correct order. They then can draw pictures of each of the products in the labelled boxes.
Support.

Key Vocabulary

environment, recycling, waste, rubbish, compact, recycle, cans, aluminium, steel, metal, recycling box, recycling centre, throw away, landfill, stages, tip

Plenary

Has this lesson made you more likely to recycle your waste?

What do you think about recycling?

Find out what you can recycle at home. Your council may have given your family some recycling boxes and there are lots of recycling banks to use near your home.

Can You Recycle? What happens to recycled drink cans?

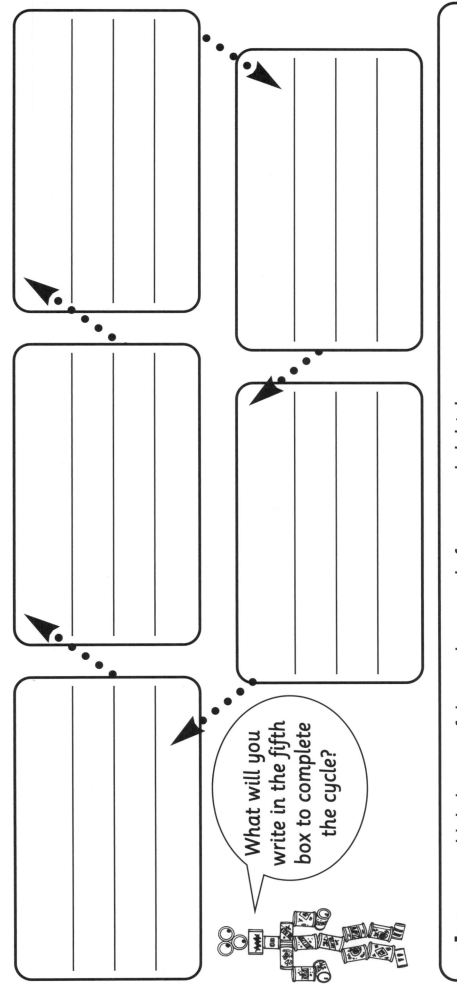

What will you write in the fifth box to complete the cycle?

* Draw and label some of the products made from recycled drink cans.

What Did They Wear?

Learning Objective

- To investigate differences between clothes that people wore in the past and now

Success Criteria

- I can draw clothes that people wore in the past and clothes that we wear today.

CD-ROM Resources

- PowerPoint file
- Slides 3, 4 and 5 in the PowerPoint file or an enlarged copy of the Resource Sheet
- Copies of the Activity Sheet

Other Resources

- Pencils and coloured pencils

Introduction

Today we are going to look back to the past when our grandparents or great-grandparents were young to see what sort of clothes they used to wear.

What clothes are modern? What do we wear today?

Tell the children that when it comes to clothes, the word 'fashion' is what we use to talk about popular styles. Fashion styles are usually grouped together in decades (a ten-year period), although there is often an overlap.

Display the top part of Resource Sheet 1 and point to the pictures of the 40s. Discuss these in detail. Explain that in those days many clothes were made at home using paper patterns and material. Here you can see a paper pattern and a picture of a child wearing the dress that was made. Fashion wasn't very exciting because it was during and after WWII and many people were poor. Also, there was a shortage (not enough) of everything, including money and material.

How are the clothes from the past different from/similar to the modern clothes we wear today?

Display the next part of the slide and discuss the pictures of the 50s clothes in detail. After the war there was more material and fashion made use of it. Clothes became brighter and more cheerful and exciting! Girls' skirts were worn with lots of petticoats to make them stick out. Boys' trousers were narrow (drainpipes) and short so you could see their brightly coloured socks. They wore long jackets (called drapes) that had velvet collars, often in bright colours, and creepers – suede shoes with huge soles. Another fashion for boys at this time was to wear a cardigan, polo shirt, longer tapered trousers and winklepickers shoes – these had very long pointed toes.

How are they different from/similar to those in the 40s/Now?

Repeat this for the 80s. There were punks who had spiky, coloured hair called the Mohawk style, and wore clothes with safety pins and piercings in their skin. Some men wore torn, bleached stained jeans and torn tee-shirts. Shoes included Dr Martens (heavy combat boots). Some people preferred what is called 'glam rock'. They wore smart suits often with big shoulder pads. And another casual outfit appeared on the scene: shell suits.

Explain the activity.

Activity

ALL ABILITIES (Differentiation is by outcome.)

- All the children should select two decades to draw outfits on their 'models'.
- The outfits can be for a male, female or one of each.
- Each outfit should be labelled with the decade from which it came.
- The third 'model' is for the children to draw an outfit that is fashionable today.
- All drawing must be done with care and colouring-in should be neat, even and within the lines they drew.
- Remind them to add facial features and hair.

Extension: The children could design an outfit for the future on the back of the sheet and label it, giving details of style and materials (according to their ability).

NB: The 'dolls' could be photocopied individually onto A4 card so that they can stand up for displaying.

Key Vocabulary

modern, new, old, before, after, grandparents, great grandparents, today, the past, decade 1940s, 1950s, 1980s, 2000, different from, similar to, fashion, fashionable, WWII

Plenary

Share as many designs as possible across the ability groups.

What decade did you choose for your 1st/2nd?

Why did you pick that outfit to draw?

What was it about the clothes that you liked?

Can you describe the outfit in detail for us?

What decade do you think had the best/worst fashions?

What clothes do you like to wear?

What do you think your grandchildren might think of your fashions in the future when you are old and they are young?

What Did They Wear?

I can draw clothes that people wore in the past and that we wear today. ☐

The Animals Went In Two By Two

Learning Objective

- To use voices expressively by singing songs, keeping to a steady pulse

Success Criteria

- I can perform 'The Animals Went In Two By Two', using words and actions.

CD-ROM Resources

- Audio file of 'The Animals Went In Two By Two'
- PowerPoint file
- Slide 4 in the PowerPoint file or an enlarged copy of the Resource Sheet

Other Resources

- CD player
- Optional:
- Classroom instruments – e.g. maracas, triangle, tambourine, guiro, bells, rain stick, chimes

Introduction

Today we are going to learn the song 'The Animals Went In Two By Two'. We will make up some actions to go with it and then perform it as a whole class.

Play the song to the class, asking them to listen very carefully.

Explain that this song is actually telling a story.

Does anyone know what story it is telling?

Noah's Ark from the Bible (Old Testament). Noah was told by God that, because people were wicked, he was going to flood Earth. He told Noah, who was a good man, to build an ark (a house boat), and only Noah, his wife, his sons and two of each animal could live on it. Then it rained for 40 days and nights and flooded the land, and the only ones safe were those on the ark. Explain that the story in the song has been changed to make it a counting song.

Display the Resource Sheet and play the song again.
Which animals went into the ark?

Explain to the children that the 'pulse' of a song is like the pulse we have in our body, a regular pattern, or beat or rhythm, that we can feel as our heart is pumping blood around. In our body, our pulse can get faster or slower depending on what we are doing. It is the same for the pulse in music. In music, speed (i.e. fast or slow) is referred to as 'tempo'.

Play a small section of the track again.
What is the tempo of the pulse in this song? Is it fast or slow?
Quite fast.

Model tapping or clapping the pulse, and then ask the children to join in, either by clapping or by tapping it out on their knees, along with the music.

Explain to the children that the pulse (or beat or rhythm) of a song shows us how to sing the lyrics (words). When we clap or tap, we are clapping or tapping on the stronger beats in the pattern of music. So, when we sing the words, we put more stress on those syllables.

Model this for the children, and then ask them to join in.

Activity

ALL ABILITIES, WHOLE CLASS, TEACHER-LED

All the children should:

- sing the first three lines of the song until they are familiar with the words and the rhythm is correct;
- learn the animal line, making sure the emphasis is on the first syllable of the animal name;
- practise the rhythm of the last line;
- sing the whole of the first verse all the way through;
- repeat the process for each verse.

Ask the children to think of some actions for each line and animal. For example, holding up the correct number of fingers for 'two by two', moving fingers up and down for rain, stamping feet heavily for the hippos, and so on.

Optional: If time, selected children (as many as possible) could use a classroom instrument to represent the animals and the rain throughout the song.

Extension: The children could be split into groups, each group singing their own animal line while the whole class sings the rest.

Key Vocabulary

pulse (tempo), tap out, clap, rhythm, voice, singing, breathing, posture, high, low, fast, slow, control, expressively

Plenary

Perform the song confidently, all the way through. If appropriate, use the classroom instruments for the performance. If possible, try to arrange for another class or a member of staff to be the audience.

Who can tap out the pulse of the song?

Who can clap the rhythm?

Who thinks they performed well with others?

The Animals Went In Two By Two

The animals went in two by two, hurrah! hurrah!
The animals went in two by two, hurrah! hurrah!
The animals went in two by two,
The elephant and the kangaroo,
And they all went into the ark,
For to get out of the rain.

The animals went in three by three, hurrah! hurrah!
The animals went in three by three, hurrah! hurrah!
The animals went in three by three,
The wasp, the ant and the bumble bee
And they all went into the ark,
For to get out of the rain.

The animals went in four by four, hurrah! hurrah!
The animals went in four by four, hurrah! hurrah!
The animals went in four by four,
The great hippopotamus stuck in the door,
And they all went into the ark,
For to get out of the rain.

The animals went in five by five, hurrah! hurrah!
The animals went in five by five, hurrah! hurrah!
The animals went in five by five,
They warmed each other to keep alive,
And they all went into the ark,
For to get out of the rain.

The animals went in six by six, hurrah! hurrah!
The animals went in six by six, hurrah! hurrah!
The animals went in six by six,
They turned out the monkey because of his tricks
And they all went into the ark,
For to get out of the rain.

The animals went in seven by seven, hurrah! hurrah!
The animals went in seven by seven, hurrah! hurrah!
The animals went in seven by seven,
The little pig thought he was going to heaven,
And they all went into the ark,
For to get out of the rain.

Learning Objective

- To recognise how our behaviour affects other people

Success Criteria

- I can try to understand why my friend upset me, so that we can stay friends.

CD-ROM Resources

- PowerPoint file
- Slides 3 and 4 in the PowerPoint file or an enlarged copy of Resource Sheet 1, pages 1 and 2 ('Harry the Hedgehog' Story)
- Slide 9 in the PowerPoint file or an enlarged copy of Resource Sheet 2 (Feelings Words)

Other Resources

- Paper
- Pencils

Introduction

Today we are going to learn that we can forgive our friends for being unkind, if we can understand why they really did it.

Display and read the story 'Harry the Hedgehog' (Resource Sheet 1, pages 1 and 2) to the class and discuss it with them, asking questions such as:

Have you ever felt as poorly as Harry?

Did someone look after you when you were poorly?

How did it feel?

Why did Gertrude give him the bell?

Why did all his friends run around for him?

Explain that friendship means looking after and caring for each other. Doing things for others, to make them happy, makes you feel good too!

Why do you think Harry pretended he was still ill and kept ringing the bell?

Paired talk for a minute, and then share reasons.

Why do you think Harry's friends forgave him?

Include that he owned up immediately, apologised and was genuinely sorry.

Why was it important that he owned up immediately?

Explain to the children that everyone makes mistakes – that is how we learn, not just in lessons, but with friendships too. It is not always easy to forgive someone, but you should always try really hard to, and carry on being friends.

Wouldn't you want your friends to forgive you?

Say that it is important to try to understand why a friend did something to be able to forgive them. How could you find out what made them do or say whatever it was that upset you? Paired talk for one minute.

Without saying any names, can you think of a time when one of your friends did or said something to you that wasn't very kind? Write some of their ideas on the board and briefly discuss with the class some possible reasons for their behaviour.

Tell the children that they will be given a scenario from the list on the board and will role-play it to show one possible reason.

Activity

ALL ABILITIES WORKING IN FRIENDSHIP PAIRS

Display Resource Sheet 2.

In their pairs, the children should role-play one reason to explain the behaviour for the scenario they have been given (from the ideas on the board), using the list of 'feelings words' on Resource Sheet 2 to help them find reasons.

Extension:

The children could follow this activity up by creating a feelings chart. Using some of the 'feelings words', ask them to copy the words and illustrate them by drawing an appropriate feelings face. Remember to include happy feelings too.

Key Vocabulary

friends, friendship, forgiveness, feelings, jealous, lonely, felt, angry, happy, sad, unhappy, upset, miserable, delighted, frightened, bothered, worried, understand, kind, unkind

Plenary

Select some pairs to show their scenarios.

What was it the friend did or didn't do or say?

Why do you think that was?

Can we think of any other reason?

Remind the children that it is important to forgive our friends, but to do that, sometimes we need to understand why they were not very kind.

How could they make it up?
List some strategies on the board.

Referring to Resource Sheet 2, explain that our feelings show on our face. Discuss what happens to our facial features when we feel different emotions. For example, our eyebrows and mouth might change shape.

Ask the children to make a pledge (promise) to stop and think about why someone has acted the way they did, and to try very hard to forgive them.

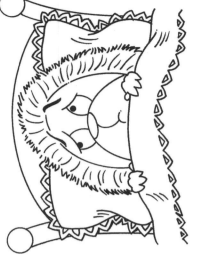

Harry the Hedgehog and His Terrible Cold

Feelings Words

upset	jealous	lonely
angry	sad	unhappy
worried	frightened	bothered

Have a Heart!

Learning Objective	Introduction	Activity	Plenary
• To recognise and describe how their bodies feel during different activities	***Today we are going to play games and think about how our bodies feel before and after being active.***	**ALL ABILITIES, WHOLE CLASS, TEACHER-LED** The children are to play several games. After each game, ask them to describe how their bodies feel, in the same way as you showed them in the Introduction.	***Can you describe how your body feels now?*** ***How is that different from before we started playing games?***
Success Criteria	***Why do our bodies need exercise?*** To keep healthy. Exercise makes our hearts go faster, pumping the blood around our bodies.	**'Spider's Web'**	Cool down:
• I can recognise and describe how my body feels during different activities.	Ask the children to concentrate on their breathing. ***Is it slow or fast? What about your heart – is it beating slowly or quickly?***	Two circles of six children are to be the spider's web, holding hands with arms in the air. The remainder of the class are flies, buzzing about (running) in and out of the web. When the teacher calls "Spider!" the web drops their arms. If a fly is caught in the trap, they are out for the remainder of the game. The game ends when the last fly is caught or the teacher calls time.	Play 'Mirrors'. The children work in pairs. One child gently stretches different body parts while the other mirrors them. After a minute ask them to swap.
Resources	***Why do we need to warm up our muscles before we exercise?*** Explain that muscles need to be gently tensed so that we don't suddenly pull them, which damages them and hurts.	**'Directions'**	Then ask the children to put their shoes on and line up to leave the hall.
• Whistle to attract attention	Ask the children to sit on the floor with their legs out straight in front of them and point their toes, then straighten their feet up again.	Tell the children they should run in the direction you point to. Verbal directions can also be given: front, behind, right and left. Once the children are used to these instructions, begin pointing in one direction and calling out another. For example, call 'Behind!' but point to the left. Eliminate children who run the wrong way or are last to reach their destination. Remind them they are to run in the direction you *point* to, not in the direction you call out, if they are different. The game ends when there is only one person left.	
For the extension: • One beanbag of each of the following colours or an A4 sheet of paper: red, orange/yellow and green	***Can you feel the muscles tense (go tight) when you point you toes, then relax (go loose) when you go back to your original position?***		
	Warm up: Play the game 'Frog and Water Shrew'. Select four or five children to be water shrews. The rest are frogs who race around on all fours, 'hopping'. The water shrews (also scampering around on all fours) must catch the frogs and 'eat them' by gently tagging their arm or leg. When caught, the frogs must lay on their backs with all four limbs up in the air until the last frog is caught or 'time' is called. Suggested length of game approximately one minute. Play again, this time choosing different shrews.	**Extension: 'Traffic Lights'** The children should run around the hall, keeping an eye on the teacher. When beanbags are held up they must react to the colour: green to run, orange/yellow to jog, red to stop.	
NB – Safety issues • Remove all jewellery and cover any earrings that cannot be removed. • Wear shoes while walking to and from the hall.	***Now concentrate on your breathing. Think about how it was before we played the game. Can you describe it now? Is it faster than before or slower? Are you out of breath? What about your heart? Can you describe what it feels like? What other changes can you feel in your body?*** Warmer, perhaps sweating, puffed out, tired.	**Key Vocabulary**	
For better class control, before leaving the classroom, set these rules: Instruct children that they will walk in single file, in silence, to the hall. When they get there, they are to find their own space and sit cross-legged and in silence. Warn them that any misbehaviour will result in them sitting out.	Explain to the children that we need to get out of breath when we play and run around. It is good for our bodies. Explain the activity.	**exercise, breathing, heart beat, muscles, relaxed (loose), tensed (tight), out of breath (puffed out), warmer, tired**	

Success Criteria

I can recognise and describe how my body feels during different activities.

✔ I can describe how my body feels before an activity.

✔ I can understand why I need to warm up my muscles before I exercise.

✔ I can describe how my body feels after an activity.

✔ I can understand why it is good for my body to get puffed out when I run around and play.

Supply Teacher Feedback Form

Class:

Supply Teacher's Name:

Date:

Class behaviour: (please circle)

| Excellent | Good | Satisfactory | Unsatisfactory/Poor |

Incidents:

Maths:

☺ Excelled:

☹ Struggled:

Literacy:

☺ Excelled:

☹ Struggled:

Other subjects:

☺ Excelled:

☹ Struggled:

Other subjects:

☺ Excelled:

☹ Struggled:

Additional information/General comments:

Signed:

Supply Teacher Feedback Form – Sample

Class: *2M* **Date:** *21/11/2009*

Supply Teacher's Name: *Candy Adler*

Class behaviour: (please circle)

(**Excellent**)   **Good**   **Satisfactory**   **Unsatisfactory/Poor**

Incidents: *Stephanie was crying when she arrived but settled down after a while.*

Maths: *To recall pairs of numbers that total 10 (and then 20)*

☺ Excelled: *Matthew, Sian, Amir, Jamal*

☹ Struggled: *Jaswinder, Luke, Jordan*

Literacy: *To compose and write simple sentences using alliteration*

☺ Excelled: *Lucy, Matthew, Amir, Jamal*

☹ Struggled: *Charlotte, Jaswinder, Luke*

Other subjects: *Science – To recognise similarities and differences between themselves and others*

☺ Excelled: *Matthew, Maya, Jamal*

☹ Struggled: *Luke, Jake*

Other subjects: *History – To investigate differences in clothes that people wore in the past and now*

☺ Excelled: *Maya, Lucy, Matthew, Sian, Amir*

☹ Struggled: *Jordan, Jaswinder*

Additional information/General comments:

I had a lovely day with your class!

Signed:

Maths

Simply Sorting

Simply Sorting

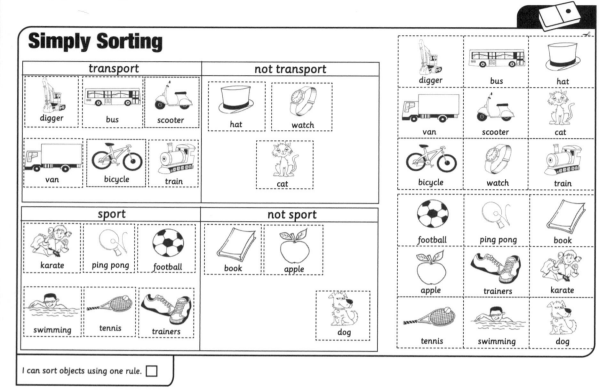

transport			not transport	
digger	bus	scooter	hat	watch
van	bicycle	train		cat

sport			not sport	
karate	ping pong	football	book	apple
swimming	tennis	trainers		dog

I can sort objects using one rule. ☐

Simply Sorting

	even numbers	not even numbers
less than 50	42 28 6	37 15 21 45
not less than 50	78 50 64	53 61

	parts of the body	not parts of the body
on the face	nose eyebrow chin mouth	glasses
not on the face	arm knee elbow ear ankle leg	sock watch

glasses   arm
nose   leg   mouth
sock   chin   ankle
watch   ear   knee
eyebrow   elbow

78   37
42   64   21
53   50   6
61   45   28
15

I can sort using 2 criteria (rules). ☐

Maths

Simply Sorting

	multiples of 10	not multiples of 10
less than 100	90 30 20 70	85 98 28 43 67
not less than 100	150 110 130	176 132

	words with an a	not words with an a
words with more than one vowel	loaf coat	poor sheep
not words with more than one vowel	bag cat mat	fox lot lip pot shirt

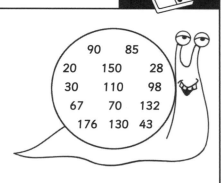

bag	fox	loaf
lot	lip	coat
pot	mat	poor
cat	sheep	shirt

I can sort using 2 criteria (rules). ☐

Shape Spotting

Shape Spotting

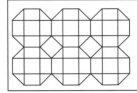

Triangle, rectangle, square, diamond (or kite), octagon
What do you notice about the diamond in the middle if you turn the pattern diagonally? Squares

Triangles 24   Octagons 6   Rectangles 24   Squares 8

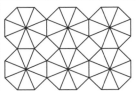

Triangle, square, diamond (or kite), octagon

What do you notice about the diamond in the middle if you turn the pattern diagonally? squares

Triangles 48   Octagons 6   Squares 2

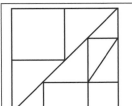

Rectangle, triangle, square

Squares 3 (including the outside)   Triangles 8   Rectangles 1

Maths

Dot-to-Dot Multiples

Dot-to-Dot Multiples

I can count on in 2s and 10s. ☐

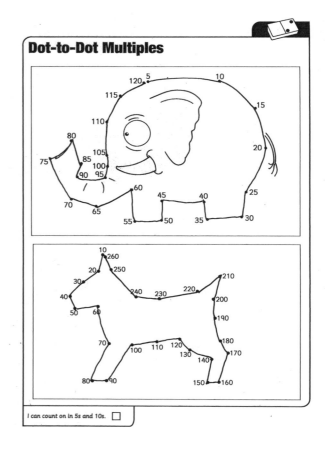

Dot-to-Dot Multiples

I can count on in 5s and 10s. ☐

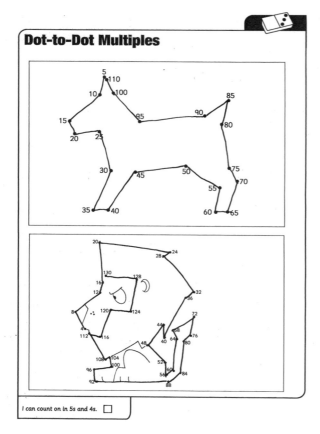

Dot-to-Dot Multiples

I can count on in 5s and 4s. ☐

Dot-to-Dot Multiples

I can count on in 1s and 2s. ☐

Literacy

Same Sound Sentences

Suggested answers

Silly Sally sang.
Hannah hopped home.
Dirty dogs dig.

Word not used: blows

Scary skinny skeletons skip.
          or: Skinny scary skeletons skip.
Greedy goblins grab grapes.
Clever clowns catch clouds.
Purple plums please people.
          or: Plums please purple people.

Word not used: wiggle

Five friends photograph funny faces.
          or: Funny friends photograph five faces.
          or: Five funny friends photograph faces.
          or: Friends photograph five funny faces.
Gentle giants juggle ginger jelly.
Little Lily licked lemon lollipops.
          or: Lily licked little lemon lollipops.
Six slim snakes slither slowly.

Words not used: crawls, munch

Literacy

Word Detective

Word Detective

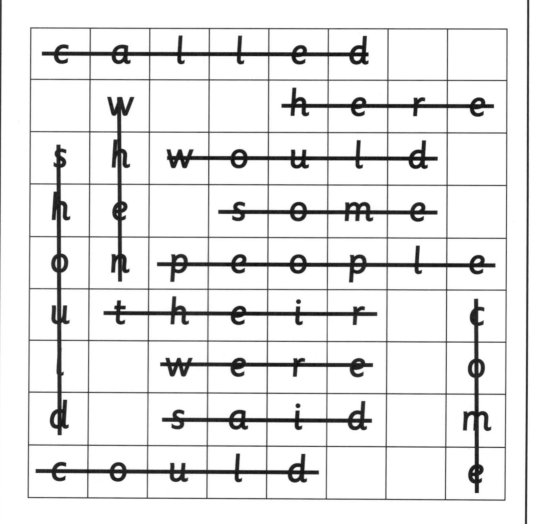

Literacy

Making Toast!

Making Toast: Instructions

How to *make toast*	

What you need
a toaster, a slice of bread, a knife, a plate, butter

What to do

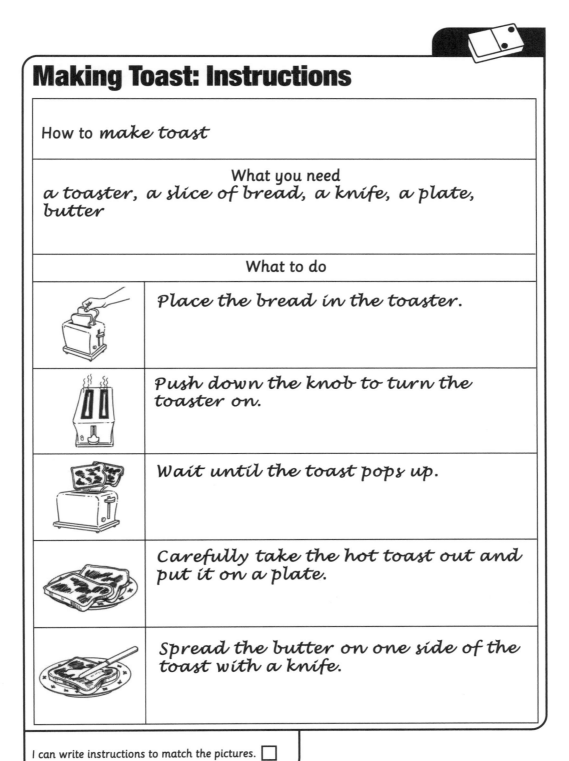	*Place the bread in the toaster.*
	Push down the knob to turn the toaster on.
	Wait until the toast pops up.
	Carefully take the hot toast out and put it on a plate.
	Spread the butter on one side of the toast with a knife.

I can write instructions to match the pictures. ☐

Literacy

A Poem About Me

A Poem About Me: Phonics Starter

Long 'e' crossword

Across
1. To shout loudly
3. Has a meal, chomps
6. You use this to unlock a door

Down
1. What you do at night, in bed
2. Myself, I
4. Someone who steals; another name for a robber
5. An insect that makes honey

¹s	c	r	e	a	²m
l					e
³e	a	⁴t	s		
e		h			⁵b
p		i			e
	⁶k	e	y		e
		f			